New York,
May 2013

To Zach & Rohan:
thank you for your time
and valuable insights.
We hope you enjoy
the book!

Maria Teresa Cometto

Alessandro H

Maria Teresa Cometto, Alessandro Piol

TECH
AND THE
CITY

foreword by Fred Wilson

THE MAKING OF
NEW YORK'S
STARTUP COMMUNITY

Mirandola Press

MIRANDOLA PRESS
TECH AND THE CITY: The Making of New York's Startup Community
Maria Teresa Cometto and Alessandro Piol

Foreword by Fred Wilson
Editor: Drew Hammond
Cover design by Sara Matiz, www.mad-nyc.com

Published in English by Mirandola Press
ISBN: 978-0-9890744-1-4

Published in Italian by Edizioni Angelo Guerini e Associati SpA

Version 1.0
Printed by CreateSpace, a division of Amazon.com

http://tech-and-the-city.com

*To Serena, Francesca and
Marco, future entrepreneurs*

CONTENTS

Foreword

By Fred Wilson, Co-founder and
Managing Partner of Union Square Ventures

Thirty years ago this summer, my wife Joanne and I graduated from college in Boston and made our way to New York City to find an apartment and start the jobs we had landed. Neither of us had ever lived in NYC. We didn't have any friends or relatives there. We had no savings, no wealth, but we had ambition. We were going to make it in NYC.

Over the past thirty years, we have made NYC our home, we have raised a family here, we have built incredible friendships here, and we have made a fortune, lost almost all of it, and made it back several times over. It has been everything we hoped for that summer and more.

This is the American dream and this is the NYC dream. This is a story that people have been telling about NYC for the past 400 years. New York City was settled by Dutch merchants looking to expand their trade. There have been fortunes made and lost in NYC ever since.

There are so many amazing things about our adopted home. I honestly can't imagine living anywhere else. But above all, NYC is hyper-evolutionary. My friend, Jason Goldman, one of the founding team members at Twitter said to me upon moving to NYC from San Francisco, that "NYC is meta unstable." He told me that he feels like the city is inherently unstable, and therefore in a constant state of implosion.

New Yorkers implicitly understand this. So the only way we can keep the city functioning is to be constantly seeking to upgrade it in real time. And that is why the city is in a constant state of construction. That's why New Yorkers are always looking for a better way to do something and a faster way to get somewhere.

This hyper-evolutionary character has allowed NYC to go from Dutch merchants trading furs, to English trading cotton, to a hub for European immigration, to the center of media, finance, fashion, and a host of other important industries. All along the way, the land and buildings of NYC have been bought and sold creating vast real estate holdings and fortunes.

So the story of NYC is a story of entrepreneurship, evolution, and energy. And it makes perfect sense that the most important industry of our time, technology, is taking hold in NYC and becoming an important force in our city.

As I write, I am staring out the window at the former Bell Labs building located between Bethune and Bank Streets on the west side of Manhattan. The digital technology industry was born in the mid 1950s at Bell Labs, when three scientists invented the transistor there. I like to start every morning by staring at that building. Because what Bell Labs unleashed on the world almost 70 years ago now is among the most transformative inventions man has ever seen.

The digital technology revolution may have started in the NYC area but it quickly moved north (to Boston) and west (to Silicon Valley) where it was rooted for its first forty years. NYC did not lead the initial phase of the technology revolution that gave us the infrastructure for everything that is now happening. But once we had a stable and ubiquitous technology stack, realized in the global Internet and devices of all shapes and sizes that seamlessly connect to it, NYC started to flex its muscle.

The story of how that came to be, how NYC started to flex its muscle in the fifth decade of the digital technology revolution, and how it may someday come to equal regions like Silicon Valley, is the story of this book. It also happens to be the story of our personal adventure. Timing is everything in life, and we made our way to NYC about a decade before the technology revolution landed in NYC, and we were ideally positioned to do something about it. And we did. And now it is time for us to reinvest.

If NYC can learn anything from Silicon Valley it is the power of plowing back the fruits of the harvest back into the soil. What I mean by that is that the culture of Silicon Valley is based on entrepreneurs reinvesting their wealth back into the next generation of entrepreneurs. Startups become big companies, the founders cash in their chips, and reinvest a good portion of that into the next startup. The same thing happens with talent. People who are hired into one startup and live through its explosive growth go on to start the next company and they hire people into their company who will start the next company in a few years.

In the first decade of the Silicon Valley story, there were maybe two or three impactful companies. In the second decade, there were maybe a half dozen. In the third decade, there were maybe a dozen. Now in the sixth decade, there might be a hundred. The Silicon Valley model has a multiplicative effect that results in ever more innovation, capital formation, wealth and growth.

NYC is adopting this model in our technology community. Now, as we embark on our third decade, we have dozens of impactful companies that have created wealth, angel investors, entrepreneurs, and talent. We are plowing the fruits of our harvest back into our soil. And we are doing more than that. We are helping the city government figure out how to train more technology talent in our public schools, we are getting the city wired, and we are pushing our city leaders to leverage the power of digital technology to make NYC more livable and more efficient.

I hope this book will be an inspiration to New Yorkers to embrace the technology revolution that has taken hold in our city. I hope it will drive our city to do more, to build more, to invest more, and to embrace everything that digital technology can do for society.

I also hope it will be an inspiration to other cities, countries, and cultures who may have missed out on the initial wave of the technology revolution. What has happened in NYC can happen anywhere that has the entrepreneurial spirit and the freedom to innovate. And just like NYC, it starts with a small number of committed individuals who see something that others do not. If you are one of those people, read on.

Fred Wilson
West Village, New York City
February 2013

Introduction

By Maria Teresa Cometto

Visit New York's Meatpacking District in the evening and you are bound to be overwhelmed by the sheer number of taxis and black limousines, the throng of girls in spike heels who stumble on the cobblestones, and the long lines of hopefuls waiting to get past the doormen of clubs. Return in the morning, and the trendiest part of New York seems to be asleep. The streets are deserted, the stores are still closed, and the protective grills on the ex-slaughterhouses that have been transformed into discos are locked tight. But this is just a façade. If you go into the restored historic buildings around Gansevoort Street with their open brickwork and steel beams on view as dictated by post-industrial chic, you find a beehive of activity: hundreds of young computer geeks. These are the protagonists of the new technological boom that is changing the economy of the city. Their ambitious goal is to make New York the new capital of high-tech.

"1,040 technological companies are hiring!" says a notice on the *Made in NY Digital Map* website on December 2, 2012. And it was not an unusual day. There really are that many high-tech companies in town, mostly startups, new businesses created in the last five years. Thanks to their dynamism, New York has recovered from the crisis of 2008 more quickly than all other

American metropolises except Houston, Texas, and Washington, D.C. Both these cities have also recovered well, but for different reasons— Houston thanks to oil, and Washington thanks to lobbyists and government workers. From 2007 to 2011 the number of jobs in the technology sector in New York increased by 28.7% from 41,100 to 52,900, while job numbers decreased in such traditionally strong sectors as finance (-5.9%); publishing (-15.8%); legal services (-7%); and manufacturing (-29.5%). At the same time the number of venture capital investments in New York startups grew by 32%, while that number fell by 10% in Silicon Valley and by 14% in Boston and surrounding areas.

New York is on its way to overtaking Silicon Valley as the center of attraction for talent and capital from all over the world, say the evangelists of the New York high-tech community. Among them are the survivors of the Internet mania of the '90s who burned hundreds of millions of dollars invested in the "dot-coms," but also created successes such as DoubleClick, the New York ad-tech company that Google bought in 2007 for $3.1 billion. And there are also new arrivals, young people who are following the American dream, not on Broadway in the hope of making it in show business, and not on Wall Street to be lured by the bonuses of investment banks, but in the digital industry that is revolutionizing the economy.

New York has already overtaken Boston in the Internet and mobile sectors, according to the *New Tech City* study published by the Center for Urban Future in May 2012. Silicon Valley is still way out front in size and accumulated experience—it is five to six times larger than New York by volume of capital invested. Hewlett-Packard, the "grandfather" of all the successive generations of California startups, was founded in 1939, and Stanford, the university-factory of so many Silicon Valley minds, was founded in 1891, while New York is only on its second or third generation of high-tech entrepreneurs. But New York is rapidly gaining ground. Beginning in 2013, it will be in an important first place: the first city in the United States to have its own "top level" Internet domain (the suffix in an Internet address such as .com or .org). The use of .nyc in web addresses by new startups will help consolidate the image of the city as a high-tech hub.

What was the spark that started the New York technological renaissance? How different is it from the California model? What can other cities and countries learn from New York as they try to promote innovation as a growth engine? Moreover, what does New York offer today to those in search of work in the high-tech sector or those who are looking to finance their business plan?

These are some of the questions that inspired this book, which is partly a love letter to the authors' adoptive city, but also a contribution to the discussion, applicable to other geographies as well, on how to leave the crisis behind and re-launch the economy. [Both authors are Italian-born New Yorkers— Alessandro has lived in New York for almost 40 years while I have lived in the city for over 12 years—and we both work in the technology field.]

To be sure, there has been much talk about startups, in the US as well as in other countries. In Italy, for instance, the Monti government recently created an ad hoc law to encourage their creation and success. But it is not enough to create an entrepreneurial ecosystem on paper. In fact, many other attempts to recreate the Silicon Valley model have failed.

In our effort to understand what is happening in New York, we spoke to over 50 key individuals—founders of the most important and interesting startups in various fields from social media to e-commerce, software, digital design and manufacturing. We spoke to "angel" investors and venture capitalists; managers of "co-working spaces," accelerators and incubators; representatives of big companies such as Google; university professors in New York City; managers of the city administration; and others. For us, it has been an exciting journey of discovery that we have organized in three sections.

The first section treats the history of the New York technological community from the euphoria of Silicon Alley in the '90s through today. During the past 15 years, the city has reeled under four heavy blows, but it has always picked itself up, confirming its special resilience. In the year 2000, the dot-com bubble "burst" for companies traded on the Nasdaq. On September 11, 2001 the city endured the terrorist attack on the World Trade Center. Then, in the fall of 2008, there was the Wall Street panic after the failure of Lehman Brothers. And, most recently, in October 2012, Superstorm Sandy devastated much of the eastern seaboard, leaving death and destruction in its wake, as well as leaving many homes and businesses without electricity (and Internet) for several days, and this included many of New York's downtown startups.

The 2008 crisis in particular became the catalyst for the current growth trend in the high-tech sector. Much of this is due to the commitment of Mayor Bloomberg, himself the founder of a startup that combines technology and finance and that has made him a billionaire. Bloomberg understood that he had to be bold, or else he would be forever known for presiding over the decline of Wall Street. As a result, he sought a third term as mayor and won, promising diversification of the local economy into sectors of the future.

His is a policy of attention and encouragement to startups; providing incentives in areas where new entrepreneurs can take their first steps—experiments in public schools as the creation of the first high school dedicated to computer science, the Academy for Software Engineering, and, above all, the challenge of the new Cornell NYC Tech University campus, concentrating on applied sciences. This is a two billion dollar project totally financed by Cornell University; but it was the brainchild of Bloomberg, who wished to respond to the chronic lack of engineers in New York, and to train a new generation of scientist-entrepreneurs to guarantee that the current technological boom should continue and grow stronger for decades. Construction of the campus on Roosevelt Island will begin in 2014 and finish in 2037. The first buildings will be inaugurated in 2017 but as early as January, 2013, the first course was held in classrooms in the huge Google building in Chelsea, which Google offered for use free of charge.

The New York headquarters of Google is one of the stops on the special tour of the Big Apple in the second section of this book. We begin in the Flatiron District and Union Square, the historic heart of Silicon Alley where one still finds the highest density of startups—entire buildings renovated so as to offer enormous open layouts such as those occupied by General Assembly. There you find hundreds of aspiring entrepreneurs who are learning the ABCs of starting their own business in the digital era and where thirty-some businesses are already taking their first steps.

The Chelsea neighborhood is dominated by Google. In 2006, Google moved into a building filling a whole city block. Few people know that over 3000 "Googlers" work there. These include engineers as well as advertising and marketing specialists who work together in a single environment. Unless one enters the premises to see it, it is difficult to have a sense of the dynamic atmosphere there, seeing the engineers dart by on scooters to get from one end of the building to the other, or overhearing their chat in the break areas. The fact that Google chose to invest so much here is one of the signs of the growing importance of New York as a center of high-tech.

Dennis Crowley is the "mayor" of Soho according to the jargon of Foursquare, one of the most famous New York startups in the world because its mobile application is used in dozens of countries besides the United States, from Britain to Turkey, from Italy to Japan. Not too far from Soho in the east

Village is the headquarters of Meetup, another well-known international trademark. The NY Tech Meetup community has thrived under its umbrella and counts over 30,000 members.

In a section of Brooklyn just over the bridge from Manhattan, you find Dumbo digital, full of online marketing and advertising agencies. Here there is also a new movement of "makers," i.e. those who make something, like the artisans of Etsy and the inventors at MakerBot.

In Queens we find Shapeways, the startup that built the "factory of the future"—a new plant to create objects using 3-D printing technology. The founder of Shapeways is a Dutch entrepreneur who moved to New York in 2010 in order to find capital and new markets. This is becoming an ever more common choice among European businesspeople.

Things are even happening in the South Bronx, thanks to the Sunshine incubator, opened in January 2012, despite the stereotypes associated with the area —one of the poorest in the United States. As for Staten Island, the best-known startup so far was Antonio Meucci's. Meucci was the Italian inventor of the telephone and his startup was a failure. A visit to his museum reminds us that even the most brilliant idea is useless unless it can find the capital to finance it.

The third part of the book is a "conversation" on themes, beginning with an analysis of the New York startup ecosystem. The fundamental ingredients of this conversation are the voices of the protagonists. They are full of talent and creativity, energy and enthusiasm, so much so that they might come across as maniacs ready to risk failure and then start over again. But they are also generous with their time, as mentors to the younger generation, and with their money to finance good ideas. Without exception, they have a strong sense of community, one they identify with and are proud of—the New Tech City where new companies have a typically metropolitan character and grow thanks to an exchange of ideas and business with other sectors as fashion and finance, media and advertising, culture and show business. It is an environment that is often friendly to women entrepreneurs. In fact, as a percentage of the total, there are twice as many startups founded by women in New York as there are in Silicon Valley or in London. And New York is also encouraging to Europeans, who find the lifestyle in the Big Apple more like that of the "old world" compared to Silicon Valley, where the prevailing culture is techno-centric and where it is impossible to live without a car.

Today the boom in New York is mostly in consumer services, where, with minimal capital, one can create a new company that leverages the professional ability of the city in the fields of design and communications. But the future is not limited to this sector, as shown by the creation of some of the first software companies to focus on business and enterprise, itself an area of special interest to the sponsors of the Cornell NYC Tech campus.

Is the current boom sustainable or are we in the middle of another euphoric bubble? Is the disappointment in Facebook's IPO and other Web 2.0 companies as Zynga and Groupon a sign that things are once again exaggerated? No, (almost) everyone replies, convinced that this euphoric phase is much more sustainable than the last because we are only just beginning to take advantage of the opportunities provided by digital and mobile technologies. There are also some people, such as Scott Heiferman, the founder of Meetup, who dream of New York as the capital of a new economy characterized by DIO as in "Do It Ourselves," where self-sufficiency reigns supreme together with peer-to-peer exchanges as alternatives to the model of mass production and consumption.

The discussion remains open and lively. Even if you only want to gather a few ideas or trends, to lose yourself in the New York technological community is an invaluable experience. How to do it is explained at the end of the book, in the guide to available resources for those who want to come to New York to study startups, work here or create their own company. Where to turn for financing, where to find space, which events to attend, what to read on the web—all this is explained at the end, together with Alessandro's valuable advice to aspiring entrepreneurs in his conclusions.

All who agreed to be interviewed for this book did so because they believe it is important to share the experience and the spirit of New York's startups, both as an occasion to think about their community, and in the hope of inspiring other cities. Many of them did so because for many years they have known and esteemed Alessandro, himself a respected member of their community.

Alessandro is a second-generation venture capitalist, and it is worthwhile to describe his background. His father, Elserino Piol, is known as a guru of high-tech and the "father" of venture capital in Italy. Elserino became a full-time venture capitalist after spending a 40-year career (1952-1996) at Olivetti, the most important IT company in Italy and, until the '90s, one of the first in Europe. Olivetti was also renowned for its industrial design: its products even are on display at New York's Museum of Modern Art. Elserino Piol is also one of the investors in the first Italian Internet service provider, Tiscali, and in other successful startups like Yoox, the e-commerce fashion site known worldwide.

When his father moved the family to New York in 1974 in order to run Olivetti's operations in North America, Alessandro began to put down American roots. He was 17, and after finishing high school at the Riverdale Country School, he was admitted to Columbia University, where he studied engineering, and where he met and fell in love with his wife-to-be, Alexandra. He also obtained a Master's degree in Computer Science. Then, in 1978, Carlo De Benedetti took over as head of Olivetti and Elserino Piol went back to Italy, but Alessandro chose to stay in New York to continue his American adventure on his own.

Although his father was in Italy, Alessandro often met up with him in New York when Elserino would make a stopover on his way to Silicon Valley or Boston on hunting expeditions for strategic investments. His new assignment with Olivetti was as head of innovation strategies, and included the company's corporate venture capital fund. "He would invite me for a drink or dinner at the Drake Hotel on 56th Street, his de-facto headquarters," recalls Alessandro, "and there I had the good luck to meet several legends of venture capital of that period such as Larry Mohr, Bill Davidow, Stu Greenfield, Ed Glassmeyer, and entrepreneurs such as Bill Foster of Stratus Computer—a company still running in Massachusetts that Intel has a stake in. Bill often told me how my father had decided to invest in Stratus after he, Bill, had sketched his idea on a napkin at Logan Airport in Boston. Getting to know these people and listening to their stories helped me understand that I wanted to go into this business too."

In 1985, after four years as a programmer working for Advanced Computer Techniques and after getting an MBA at Harvard, Alessandro went to work for AT&T. AT&T's research and development arm was at Bell Labs in Murray Hill and Holmdel, New Jersey, among the most important centers of applied science in the world. Alessandro managed to get a job where he could spend time at Bell Labs, discovering an inventor's paradise.

"Their philosophy was to create, sometimes with no deadlines and no urgency to transform discoveries into saleable products. That was the beauty of a monopoly: being able to finance pure research and passing the cost down to its customers. This luxury eventually became an impossibility when AT&T was broken up after the antitrust settlement of 1983 and the subsequent deregulation of the telecom industry in order to create a competitive market."

In 1991, on behalf of AT&T and together with Bill Elliott and Neal Douglas, Alessandro started AT&T Ventures, the company's corporate venture capital fund, and so took on his first responsibilities as an investor. "In order to get some deal flow, I would fly out to Silicon Valley to meet up with investors like Vinod Khosla, one of the founders of Sun Microsystems and already a star of the VC industry at Kleiner, Perkins, Caufield and Byers," says Alessandro. "My wife, who was herself in the venture capital business and was at the time on the board of Nexgen with Vinod, introduced me to him. She managed Olivetti's portfolio here in the States from 1986 to 1995, and so had a good network in Silicon Valley. And in 1992, together with Khosla, I made my first investment in the games company Spectrum Holobyte, later bought by Hasbro."

"Most of the opportunities were on the West Coast but I wanted to stay in New York," explains Alessandro. "Those were the years when cable companies were deploying the new digital infrastructure and there was a lot of talk about interactive TV, thanks to the novel availability of two-way communications. So I called a friend of mine from Harvard, Brian Bedol, who had been in the TV industry for many years. He worked with the creator of MTV, Bob Pittman, then with Time Warner and its subsidiary, Six Flags, and in 1992 he branched out on his own. I asked him if he had any business ideas he was thinking about, and he mentioned three—a channel for teenage girls, an interactive shopping channel, and one for nostalgic sports fans. We decided that the third was the most viable as the rights to old sporting events were inexpensive while the potential number of viewers was vast. We figured many of the viewers would be fathers who wanted their kids to see one of 'their teams" historic games." And so Classic Sports Network was born, based in New York. Bedol's business partner was Stephen Greenberg, who was the former deputy commissioner of Major League Baseball and son of Hank Greenberg, the legendary baseball player. Financing was from AT&T Ventures, Allen &

Co. and Chieftain Capital. "Broadcasting began on Direct TV in 1994 and was an immediate success," Alessandro remembers. "Disney bought the channel in 1998 and today it is called ESPN Classic. AT&T made ten times its total investment."

1994 was also the year Alessandro co-founded the New York New Media Association (NYNMA), the first attempt to promote the city's technological community from the bottom up. "I was one of the fifty 'notables' in high tech invited to take part in the first event organized by Brian Horey and Mark Stahlman," says Alessandro. "At the end of the event they asked who wanted to be on the NYNMA board and have a say in running the association. I said I was interested, along with several others, and saw the organization grow for the next several years. Many of the people involved in NYNMA became protagonists of the second wave of the industry. A case in point is Dawn Barber, who then went on to co-found the NY Tech Meetup."

After leaving AT&T at the end of 1995 and working for Chancellor Capital Management, then acquired by Invesco, Alessandro is now at Vedanta Capital, a firm he co-founded with two partners in 2006. And he still works with the local tech community.

It is an open, welcoming community to those who come here following their dream. We talk about many of these people in this book—young people from India, Holland, Slovenia, Israel, Italy, Britain, and many regions of the US. We thank them and all the others who shared their stories and their thoughts.

Maria Teresa Cometto,
February 2013

I

History

A Twenty-Year Journey to Today

1
Silicon Alley
The Dot-Com Boom

What's the hottest show in New York, consistently drawing a full house? It is not on Broadway but in a theater at New York University's Skirball Center, steps from Washington Square Park. The show plays every month before an audience of 850 enthusiastic fans, who show up to admire and applaud some very special "actors": entrepreneurs who founded technology startups in the Big Apple and who take the stage to demonstrate their ideas and reveal how they are translating them into businesses. It's organized by NY Tech Meetup, and every time about 10 startups present, each with a five minute "demo": words and pictures prepared with great care, to capture the attention of potential investors who have come to hunt for new business opportunities. But the demos are also for all the other spectators—engineers, technologists, consultants, competitors—anyone interested in learning about new technologies, sometimes because they are looking for a job, or perhaps because they are looking to be inspired by these ideas to come up with an even better creation. Two intense hours, full of energy and excitement!

At the event of June 5, 2012, the evening was opened by a video that immediately achieved cult status on the Internet. The protagonist was 37-years old Michael Lazerow, founder, with his wife Kass, of Buddy Media. An amusing name for a serious and profitable business: software to manage a corporation's presence on social platforms such as Facebook and Twitter. Salesforce.com had just purchased Buddy for $689 million dollars: a killing for a five-year old New York startup. Lazerow wanted to celebrate by sharing a little known episode in his personal history, and launch a strong message to all other aspiring entrepreneurs. Suffering from heart disease from birth, he almost died at 19 when a valve stopped working. A miraculous operation saved him, and when he woke up, he remembered feeling a "deep calm" and, since then, having no fear of dying. "It's not a coincidence that I started my first company at Northwestern later that year," continued Lazerow. "13 years later, I started my fourth, Buddy Media. And 2 hours ago I signed a deal to sell it. Gandhi said that the true enemy is fear, not hatred. If you live without fear, anything is possible." Then the pitch: "Is fear holding you back?"[1]

A roaring applause erupted in the hall. All in tune with that emotional vibration, that fearlessness and love for "impossible" challenges. The temerity, some might say, that holds together the New York high-tech community: animal spirits for the third millennium. And their point of reference is the NY Tech Meetup: with over 30,000 members (as of February, 2013), it continues to grow and organize monthly events. Something like a debutante ball attended by all the successful startups such as Foursquare and Tumblr. And also an important opportunity for networking at the party that breaks out after the "demos," in a lounge adjacent to the theatre, where the beer flows, graciously offered by many sponsors.

There was always beer but, back in the day, they had to pay for it. There were few attending the first parties of NY Tech Meetup's ancestor, the New York New Media Association. NYNMA was founded in 1994 by venture capitalist Brian Horey and by Mark Stahlman, a former Wall Street technology analyst.[2]

"The initial meeting was in my loft on Duane Street, in Tribeca," says Stahlman, who is now 64 and lives in Brooklyn, "two Subway stops beyond the hipsters": in other words, in Bushwick, still on the "fringe" and not as fashionable as Williamsburg. For some a "futurist,"[3] for others a gadfly, Stahlman is emblematic of the technological community of those years, a combination of the most bizarre characters, along with serious engineers, investors and media professionals, all intellectually curious and interested in understanding how the Internet—newly available to the public—would change the traditional ways of doing business. And to begin the story of "Silicon Alley" with Stahlman is appropriate because he invented the term to evoke the growing technology landscape among the skyscrapers of Manhattan.

Born in Boston, the son of two professors, and raised in Wisconsin, in an environment "full of socialists and radicals," Stahlman graduated with a Bachelor's degree in Philosophy at the University of Wisconsin in Madison. After studying Theology at the University of Chicago and Molecular Biology back in Wisconsin, he moved to New York "to start a revolution." And in New York he met more fanatics, not only of the revolution, but also of technology. They introduced him to computers and software, leading him to start his first business. Then from 1985 to 1992 he put to good use his computer expertise on Wall Street: first as an analyst for the research firm Sanford C. Bernstein, becoming famous for recommending the shares of Sun Microsystems against the opinion of the majority of his colleagues; and then as a partner at the investment bank Alex. Brown & Sons, for which he followed the Initial Public Offering of America Online in March 1992. Well off thanks to the success of the IPO, but sick of his life as an investment banker, in the summer of that same year Stahlman decided to take some time for vacation and reflection. He donned the role of "guru" in the nascent high-tech community of New York. Along with his girlfriend, Candice Eggerss, he started the "CyberSalon," a coterie of technology enthusiasts who met once a month in his Tribeca loft and, after a bite and some beer or wine, discussed the future of media and technology. "We sat in a circle and everyone had to express his or her opinion, but my suspicion is that many of my friends came just to have an excuse to leave their homes, and then visit their mistresses after the meeting," confides Stahlman, who likes to impress his interlocutors with provocative volleys.

One of the friends was Horey, who, after a couple of years, proposed to switch from CyberSalons to "Cybersuds," a less formal networking event with the aim of bringing together the nascent "new media" community. "With NYNMA we were hoping to attract more people, so we decided to have the Cybersuds in a public place," says Stahlman. "We chose El Teddy's, a Mexican bar and restaurant in Tribeca known for its potent margaritas and cocktails and for the giant replica of the Crown of the Statue of Liberty on the roof. They would let us use their upstairs lounge, making us pay only for the drinks we consumed at the bar. But we were so few that after a few meetings they kicked us out because we couldn't generate enough business for them!"[4]

It was a slow takeoff—though the first Cybersuds attracted some interesting luminaries such as Jaron Lanier, scientist and virtual reality pioneer, who in 1990 had come back from California to New York City, where he was born 30 years earlier. With him, the debate could go from philosophical, about how digital technology could enrich human interaction, to the arts, taking a cue from his other great passion, the "new classical music" performed with rare and exotic instruments he liked to collect and display in his apartment on the same street as Stahlman's.

"Nobody believed that New York was the right place for technology business" remembers Stahlman. "When I went to Albany to apply for New York State funding for NYNMA, officials of the economic development agency took me for a scammer and asked me in which Caribbean island I was planning to escape with the cash."

But in less than a year, cyber-fever would infect even the Big Apple, and at the end of '95—the year of Netscape's IPO, the company that commercialized the first browser and promised "web for all," doubling its share value on the first day of trading—NYNMA had reached 1,700 members. And Cybersuds had become the "coolest" party in Manhattan: held at the Roxy, a nightclub in Chelsea, with 600 participants in an atmosphere full of "excitement" and "adrenaline" similar "maybe only to when the TV was invented," according to *New York* magazine in an issue dedicated to the "High-Tech Boom Town."[5]

"Before '95, I couldn't explain to a regular person what I was doing for a living," says Cella Irvine, one of the original board members of NYNMA and eventually its President. "I was working at Prodigy, a joint venture between IBM and Sears, which since the late '80s was offering an interactive online service. But few understood what it meant. In New York we were a small community of people, joined by a feeling that we were doing something exciting and pioneering. But if you wanted to have any technology work done, you had to go to California, in Silicon Valley. It was a running joke that you could find the board of NYNMA by walking onto the two o'clock flight from San Francisco to New York on any given Friday, because we all had to travel back and forth."

"Everything changed in 1995," says Irvine, who, since October 2011, serves as CEO of Vibrant, a New York online agency specializing in contextual advertising. "Suddenly everyone seemed to know what 'interactive' meant. I remember a party in the Hamptons, where I heard some guy introducing himself as a new media executive. And I said 'Really? Me too. Where do you work?' And he replied with a laugh, 'Oh, no, I was just making it up so that I would sound good!' It was an early sign that the Internet was 'in' and would eventually lead to irrationality and excesses."

"1995 was my debut on the Internet," said Kevin Ryan, who that year placed the foundation for the most celebrated success story of Silicon Alley: DoubleClick. "I was working for United Media, and we owned the rights to comic strips, crossword puzzles and editorial columns sold to newspapers," Ryan continues. "That industry was turning into a very bad business. When there are five newspapers in a city, and we have the only comic strip, they all compete for that strip; but when there's only one newspaper in town, obviously the power changes. The price of a comic strip went from $300 a week in the 1940s to $10 a week 40 years later. So I thought I'd reach out directly to consumers: I launched an Internet site dedicated to the popular comic strip Dilbert, and it worked. After a year the site was one of the ten most visited in America and made a profit, thanks to advertising. I realized that the Internet was the most amazing trend I had ever seen. So I went to ask the managers of United Media to give me a few million dollars to create an entire online business. But they refused because they believed it was too risky and that it would cannibalize their traditional activities. That's when I decided to leave and start my own Internet company. I thought that advertising was the currency of the Internet—an intuition that would eventually prove right, while back then no one believed in it."

Quitting United Media in early 1996, Ryan looked for technology partners and found them in Dwight Merriman and Kevin O'Connor, a pair of engineers who had just founded

DoubleClick. "They created a fantastic technology to advertise online and I decided to join them, first as the President and then as CEO of DoubleClick," says Ryan. "When I joined the company we were 20 employees. Four years later we had grown to 2,000 with a presence in 25 countries: the largest New York-based Internet company."

"DoubleClick welcomes you to Silicon Alley," read a huge billboard near the Flatiron Building, after the February 23, 1998, IPO that valued Ryan's company at $270 million—about nine times its revenue. On its first day of trading, the shares shot upward by 70%, despite the company's lack of profits. Indeed, the company's bottom line was in the red, and it would remain as such for the following year in order to finance the company's growth, Ryan had explained at the time of the IPO.

Besides its importance to Ryan, 1996 was also a milestone year for Fred Wilson, venture capitalist and one of the most authoritative voices of Silicon Alley. "1996 was the year that New York City's startup community took off, and the year that the commercial Internet took off. It was a big year and an inflection point in my life," wrote Wilson 16 years later on his highly followed blog, AVC. "It was also the year that Jerry Colonna and I started Flatiron Partners," he continues in his post of June 2012. "I had been working closely with SoftBank Corporation of Japan on an investment in a company called FreeLoader, founded by Mark Pincus and Sunil Paul. When we sold FreeLoader, SoftBank approached me about joining their investment team in the US. I convinced SoftBank that there was going to be a lot of Internet startup activity in NYC and that backing me and Jerry to start a firm in NYC was a good idea. Jerry thought we might be better off with two backers instead of one (he was right), and we went to Chase Bank and got them to join the project. That's how Flatiron came to be. SoftBank, Chase, Jerry and I were the four partners in Flatiron when we got started. SoftBank was just coming onto the scene in the US. Their founder and CEO Masayoshi Son was on the cover of *Business Week* that summer of 1996."[6]

"I don't think we had really figured out the Internet business models then, and even the basic building blocks needed to create an Internet business didn't exist at the time," says Wilson today. "Everybody was making it from scratch, and people spent millions and millions of dollars to start something. The bubble became unsustainable—the dollars spent, the little revenue produced ... the math just didn't work."

A skeptic, even a sharp critic of the first Silicon Alley that he largely avoided, but later a protagonist of the rebirth of the Internet, Don Katz is a journalist and bestselling author who, in 1995, decided to start a company of his own: Audible, the leading company in digital audiobooks. "When Silicon Alley began, I did not want to be associated with the companies that were part of it; I did not like how they structured themselves; I did not like their work ethic; I did not like that they were hiring all those fat cats from media companies and paying them a lot of money and giving them stock options," says Katz today. "I remember not going to the events, because they were not real companies, they were a bunch of ad agencies, basically, with human capital as their stock in trade; there was no real technology, there were some consulting companies, but those were services to big corporations that did not seem scalable to me. And if you look at Jason Calacanis' Silicon Alley 100 list, and fast forward to today, most of those companies are dead."[7]

One of Audible's strengths from the beginning was the technology invented to realize Katz's original vision: to free the words from printed paper and allow them to reach the public in the most usable way possible, that is via audio, taking advantage of the Internet as a distribution channel. At a time when there were only magnetic tape audiocassettes, and four years before

Apple's launch of the iPod, Audible created the first portable player to play sounds downloaded from the Internet. The Smithsonian Museum in Washington, DC, still displays it as an important piece of new media history.

Born in 1952 in Chicago, an NYU graduate with a Master's degree from the London School of Economics, Katz left behind a 20-year career as a journalist—with the magazines *Rolling Stone* and *Esquire*—and as a bestselling author with books such as *Just Do It*, narrating the rise of Phil Knight and his Nike empire,[8] and other works. Doing research for a book on new technologies, he became enthusiastic about the Internet and how you could distribute data, including spoken words, through the network. And he had imagined that the book market could be revolutionized by the new medium. Approximately 100 million Americans drive the car to go to work every day, and this is only a slice of the potential audience who could listen to books while engaged in something else, Katz figured. From the outset he decided to open Audible's headquarters not in New York, the American capital of media, but in New Jersey, the "Garden State" to the West of New York: at first near his home in Montclair, and eventually in Newark, just across the Hudson river from Manhattan.

"I chose New Jersey also because a lot of tech talent was out in this Jersey corridor, arguably more than there was at that point in New York City. Our CTO Guy Story, for instance, comes from Bell Labs and many other engineers also came from Bell Labs," Katz says. "To me New York is not hipster heaven. All the dinosaurs that we are changing are in New York. It is a bunch of old Lunchtime O'Booze publishing executives who arrogate to be the industry when they have never invented or done anything. All innovations in the book business—the paperback book, the book club, the superstore, the discounters, Amazon, Audible—were all created outside the industry: it was never organic. A process similar to what occurred in music and cinema. In short, content guys are not very progressive." And staying a few miles away from Silicon Alley, Katz grew Audible until in 2008 Amazon.com acquired it for $300 million, leaving it independent under his leadership.

"It's true, after 1996, the atmosphere was heating up in Silicon Alley, everyone wanted to invest and startup valuations were beginning to rise quickly," confirms Alain Bankier, a Franco-American businessman born in 1955 in Casablanca, Morocco, graduate in economics and psychology from the University of Pennsylvania and the Wharton School, and with an MBA in finance from New York University and HEC School of Management in Paris. Until 2001 he was responsible for North America corporate finance for the French group BNP, to whom he had sold in 1989 his M&A boutique, Vendôme & Company. "When in the mid-'90s I realized the scope of the Internet, I went to BNP with a business plan to create a special technology corporate finance group," says Bankier. "But they responded 'No, we don't believe that this Internet thing is going to work. It's American marketing hype. We'll stick with Minitel,'" referring to the French information service provided via home terminals connected to a telephone line, which was finally shut down on June 30, 2012. "Then I asked permission to invest on my own, in my spare time and separately from them. And I started looking around." Attracting his attention was, among other content-based startups, Nerve.com, founded in 1997 by Rufus Griscom and Genevieve Field with the slogan "literate smut."

"They were doing literature with an erotic twist. I thought, people are going to like that," recalls Bankier. "It was one of my early investments. Nerve.com still exists and continues to generate revenue (with personal ads, premium subscriptions, book publishing and advertising). It survived the dot-com crash of 2000 because Rufus was able to manage a lean company: he had raised little money and squeezed the most out of it, careful to quickly drop the projects that were not working." Ultimately Nerve created and spun out babble.com, a leading parenting site that was sold to The Walt Disney Company in 2011. Bankier was an investor in other New York digital media pioneers such as Total New York, founded by John Borthwick in 1994, and is also an investor in Borthwick's current company, Betaworks.

In '97 Bankier was also one of the founders of NYNMA Angels, the angel investor group associated with NYNMA, that eventually morphed into the New York Angels. "There was a lot of interest, but also a great deal of disbelief around the new technologies"—continues Bankier, now CEO of the Manischewitz Company, the well-known kosher food producer and distributor. "Young people today have grown up with the Internet, while we in the '90s didn't really understand its full potential. In addition, the technology was expensive and the Internet had not been adopted by a wide enough audience to sustain the business models of the startups of that era, among which the prevailing mentality was 'let's start, and then we'll see how to make sales and profits.' So we arrived to 2000 and 2001, with a difficult situation and I started to shut down or sell businesses so that when the bubble burst I was not stuck with too many investments."

2
Angels in New York
Collapse and the Birth of a Community

It is a morning in October 2000. At the counter of McDonald's on Broadway in NoHo, a skinny and bespectacled fellow serves burgers and fries. Long brown hair, a faint smile, can't tell whether spontaneous or in deference to the corporate policy "we love to see you smile." He is 28 years old, and was born in Homewood, a suburb of Chicago, the son of shopkeepers. He has a degree in Business, not from an Ivy League school, but from the University of Iowa. He is not, however, one of the many young people on the hunt for good luck in the Big Apple, resigned to do menial chores while they dream of becoming famous theater actors or millionaire rock stars.

In fact, he already is a millionaire. His name is Scott Heiferman and in 1995 he founded i-Traffic, a pioneering online advertising agency. In 1999, with the company employing 100 people, he sold it for $25 million (according to Crain's New York Business' estimates) to Agency.com. On December 8th of that year, Agency.com completed an IPO on Nasdaq. The debut on the stock exchange was overwhelming: the stock almost tripled on the first day, from $26 to $76 amid a euphoria that seemed unstoppable. Ten months later it would plummet to $10, overcome as all other dot-coms by the burst of the Internet bubble. Heiferman was still Chairman of a division of Agency.com and his wealth had not been completely wiped out. Why then was he working for a few dollars an hour at a fast food chain?

"I was lost, I did not know what I was most passionate about and what I wanted to do," Heiferman says today at the offices of his new venture, Meetup, just three blocks from that McDonald's. "I needed to cleanse the palate after the hangover of the fake versions of Internet businesses, until then focused on marketing and advertising." Heiferman had gone into that business in a counterintuitive way. "I was interested in changing it, even killing it," he says. "I thought that advertising was evil, in a sense, and that if it could be re-invented in the Internet age, I wanted to be the one reinventing it." Thus i-Traffic was born and Heiferman was lucky to sell it at the top of the first Internet craze. The bursting of the Bubble for him was not a tragedy but a kind of "cleansing" of insane Internet businesses.

"In 2000 when the bubble burst, it blew up Wall Street with its exaggerated valuations, and unfortunately destroyed even some good startups," notes Heiferman. "But the real underbelly and soul of the Internet, how it changes people's lives and empowers them, that never went away. In fact it was after the bubble burst that the good part of the Internet really started to take off. That was when the emergence of blogs or the emergence of phenomena such as Wikipedia, or Google and eBay, started empowering people in lots of ways. That said, I was sad to see the spectacle of dot-coms in freefall in the stock market and then failing." At McDonald's Heiferman had somehow sought to reconnect himself to his roots and the "real" world. "I grew up in a retail family where my father and grandfather ran a small paint store. Business was simple: face to face with customers, giving them good service." His first experience with high-tech was, as a kid, programming an Apple II computer to manage the store's inventory. "Then, instead, my career took an absurd turn, intensely dealing with advertisers and lawyers and bankers, in this kind of world where I did not know if we were helping anyone," continues Heiferman. "For this reason, probably in a fit of insanity, I decided to go work at McDonald's, to remind myself what it means to deal with customers, and what people are willing to pay for."

The follies of the Internet in Silicon Alley had really reached bizarre heights. Stephan Paternot, "the CEO in plastic pants," and Josh Harris, the big brother of the experiment "Quiet: We Live in Public," are the two most emblematic characters of that period.

In 1994 Paternot had founded with a college classmate theGlobe.com, a kind of primitive social network. The startup had completed an Initial Public Offering at the end of 1998 with a valuation of $840 million and a record performance, up 606%, in the first day of trading. Suddenly wealthy at 24 years of age, with a personal fortune of $100 million, based on the face value of his stock, Paternot was given to such an excessive lifestyle that in 1999 the television network CNN decided to film one of his nights out on the town. In the video he is seen sheathed in gleaming leather pants, dancing on the table in a nightclub and declaring: "Got the girl. Got the money. Now I'm ready to live a disgusting, frivolous life." So he had earned the nickname of "CEO in plastic pants." Two years later, when the bubble burst, shares of theGlobe.com went from their top of $97 to just 10 cents.[1]

Harris, instead, had founded in 1994 Jupiter Communications, a research company specializing on the Internet, and from its IPO in '99 he had earned about $10 million, soon burned with his second startup, Pseudo.com, and his experiments with TV via the Internet. The most spectacular was the creation of an underground "City" in Manhattan, in December 1999, where over 100 volunteers agreed to be filmed 24 hours a day in every aspect of their lives, even on the toilet or having sex. A "cultural provocation" about the destruction of privacy in the Internet age, it was interrupted on New Year's eve, 2000, by an NYPD raid. But one can still see it all today in the documentary *We Live in Public,* which won an award at the Sundance Film Festival in 2009.[2]

While the Nasdaq Index dropped from its historical record of over 5,048 touched on March 10, 2000, to about the 3,700 level at the end of that year, and then down to 1,108 on October 10, 2002, Wall Street did everything to try to support the stocks of dot-com companies, including continuing to churn out "Buy" recommendations.

One of the most brilliant analysts in formulating them was Henry Blodget, recruited by the investment bank Merrill Lynch, after correctly forecasting, in October 1998, that Amazon.com shares would rise from $240 to $400 (a target reached within four weeks). But what Blodget recommended in public did not always correspond to his true views expressed in private, as shown in a series of emails from the year 2000, released two years later by then New York Attorney General Eliot Spitzer, as part of an investigation into conflicts of interest by the big investment banks. "I can't believe what a POS [piece of sh..] that thing is. Shame on me/us for giving them any benefit of the doubt," wrote Blodget about LifeMinders.com, presented publicly as "an attractive investment." And 24/7 Media, on which he had an "accumulate" recommendation: "Is this a POS? Yes." These emails then cost Blodget his career as a research analyst on Wall Street, when the Securities and Exchange Commission banned him for life.

Unfairly, according to Kevin Ryan, who in 2007 chose Blodget to be the CEO of the news and commentary website *Business Insider.* "I was on the other side and saw what the other investment banks were doing, and they were all doing the same thing," says Ryan, who at the time was CEO of DoubleClick.

"Every single one of the investment banks told me 'we'll do research reports for you if you do business with us,' and that was the central problem of the whole thing. Henry got in trouble ironically because he was complaining about what was going on." The pressure investment banks were exerting on their analysts—encouraged to support companies likely to earn fees through IPOs and other financial transactions—was fueling a vicious cycle: the yeast to that speculative bubble that, bursting, destroyed much of Silicon Alley. An event that Blodget himself had indeed expected, warning several times, in public and even during the boom years, that 75% of Internet companies would fail.

But a far more devastating tragedy still was to befall New York and Silicon Alley: the terrorist attack of September 11, 2001. An absolute evil that, however unintentionally, generated a good seed.

Heiferman: "I was on a bus, going from the East Village to my house in NoHo that morning. I heard the news on the radio of the first aircraft hitting the Twin Towers and I decided to go on the roof of my apartment building. I arrived a few seconds after the second plane had hit. And then I lived through this experience I often talk about, of having more conversations and talking to more people in the hours and days after 9/11 than I had in all my previous years in New York. And that was intriguing because until then I had no particular interest in my local community. After 9/11, I became interested in the simple pleasure of talking to neighbors, to get to know them. And I understood how powerful people can be when they get organized. In those days we saw lots of vigils and support groups and I became interested in how people can get to know more neighbors, how in the future they could organize local communities about anything, and that led to Meetup: use the Internet to organize individuals in a community. A concept that then, well ahead of Facebook and the emergence of the term 'social media,' seemed ridiculous."

Meetup.com, born in 2002 and now the world's largest network of local interest groups, with over 11 million members in 45,000 cities in 2012, and profitable for the past three years, is just one of the new ideas and businesses arising from the rubble of the "first" Silicon Alley and the Twin Towers.

"After the collapse, people started to make sense of the Internet," notes Wilson. "The foundational tools got built, and people started to figure out what business models made sense and what business models didn't. Some important technologies were developed in those years, such as Google search. Even Napster had an important role because it showed people the importance of peer-to-peer systems that eventually led to the creation of platforms such as Skype. We usually refer to the years from 2000 to 2005 as the aftermath of the bubble. In reality a lot of the most important work that was done in the development of the Internet was done in that period."

"When the bubble burst it was horrible. There were many people who suffered from that, but the companies that started emerging in 2002 and 2003 were much more interesting companies than those that were getting started in 2000," confirms John Borthwick, at that time responsible for new product development for AOL, to whom he had sold his first startup, Web Partners, in 1997.

"It is natural that innovation passes through these cycles of boom and bust, to some extent driven by our capital infrastructure that tends to overinvest, feeding the system too much money and then starving it," continues Borthwick, today CEO of Betaworks, a company he founded in 2007. "In 2000 there was too much capital and it wasn't forcing entrepreneurs to work hard and ask themselves the big and hard questions about how to change the world. It was too easy. People would just add '.com' at the end of any name—shirts.com, socks.com, pants.com —and they thought it would be sufficient. Socks.com could maybe change the world, but you probably have to think about more than just selling socks. Amazon.com has changed the world and they started off as books.com, but then they figured out how to sell more than just books."

Maintaining the hope to "change the world" after the collapse of the markets and the Towers were the "angels." "A group of madmen who think they are God's gift to humanity," jokes 55-year old David S. Rose. He is one of them and was the founder in 2004, along with Howard Morgan and others, of the New York Angels as an independent group, spun out from NYNMA, which had in the meantime been merged with the Software and Information Industry Association (SIIA).

The angels are groups of small investors who typically write $25-50,000 checks each, to a startup in its nascent stage. The New York Angels are over 100 and collectively invest between $100,000 and one million dollars into a business. They gather together, each month, to listen to the presentation of new ideas by young entrepreneurs, whose business plans are then evaluated by a committee; then each individual "angel" decides whether to make an investment in an opportunity deemed deserving. Since 2004 the New York Angels have invested around 45 million and have pledged to mentor "great young companies," sometimes in collaboration with other organizations or the city's business school programs.

The angels differ from venture capitalists, who invest in companies at a more advanced stage and with higher investment commitments, usually $1 million and up, depending on the stage of the investment. Unlike individuals, venture capitalists operate through investment funds, with money raised mostly from institutions, such as pension funds, and must give a detailed account of the fund's performance.

"The nuclear winter following the dot-com crash was actually a golden age for us angels," says Rose. "Valuations of technology companies were dropping like rocks and the VCs fled the business. They had raised these huge funds, and their Limited Partners wanted their money back and were frightened. 'Don't you dare invest in that Internet stuff,' they were saying. The sector was paralyzed. But innovation does not stop. It opened great opportunities for angel investors who were, depending on your point of view, lunatic enough or smart enough to seize them. There were a bunch of successful companies that came out of that."

Rose mentions Pond5, founded in 2006, that today has become one of the largest stock video libraries on the Internet: an exchange market not only for videos, but also music, photos and special effects, where artists set the price for their products—an alternative model to the typical royalty deal, and convenient to both buyers and sellers. "Tom Bennett, the CEO of Pond5, together with his partners, founded the company, built the web site and started taking in revenues...all on an initial investment of $25,000 dollars: the world has changed, I told myself," says Rose, who led the New York Angels' investment in the startup. "Tom is the quintessence of the new era of low startup costs and rational valuations for startups. New York Angels members invested $500,000 in the company five years ago, and it has been profitable ever since."

A touch of madness and a lot of money—generated by their own businesses or occasionally inherited by family—are the common characteristics of the angels in New York. All of them, however, have a very personal story about how they started their career as an investor. Rose's story is made of exciting discoveries and depressing failures. "I come from generations of entrepreneurs," he says. "My great uncle was one of the first tech angel investors in the world: the main street at the

Technion University's campus in Israel is David Rose Avenue. I, instead, had graduated in Urban Planning from Yale, then I went to work for the Government, but I soon realized that it wasn't my path. I understood that the government can only seek to guide the economy and society at the margin, but the real engine that makes everything run is commercial entrepreneurship. So I went to Columbia Business School for my MBA and then I joined my family real estate business for a decade—Rose Associates was founded by my grandfather and my uncle in 1928 in New York."

But Rose's real passion had always been technology. He proudly shows his picture in the January 1983 Time Magazine issue dedicated to the computer as "Machine of the year 1982," where he is cited as one of the pioneers in the use of the PC, having created the first real estate management software for the personal computer.[3] His first "invention" goes back to 1988: the WristMac, a watch you could upload data to, from a Macintosh computer, used by NASA in a space mission, but too expensive to commercialize. The first marketable product, made with his startup AirMedia, was the NewsCatcher in 1996: a small pyramid-shaped device that, attached to the PC, provided news, e-mail and stock quotes gathered wirelessly through the paging network. "The idea was that the Internet was too slow in those years and the investors liked it: Lionel Pincus of the venture capital firm Warburg Pincus believed in it," remembers Rose. "But the only slight problem was that no one bought the product! Eventually we had to reorganize the company under Chapter 11, the most depressing day of my life."

But it was 1998, the Internet was booming and Rose successfully revived AirMedia, turning it into a multi-national hub for marketing over wireless networks. "Everything was going wonderfully until, in the middle of the dot-com meltdown, our major investor walked away from a $30 million follow-on round 10 days before the scheduled closing. By the fall of 2001, the writing was on the wall, and I finally closed it for good. My wife grounded me: 'enough of this entrepreneurial stuff!' And I was sitting there licking my wounds," reminisced Rose. "Till when, in 2002, I decided to invest in other people's startups and became an angel."

But Rose never abandoned his dream of creating his own successful company: the year after he started—with Howard Morgan, Josh Kopelman, Esther Dyson, Scott Kurnit and other active investors—the New York Angels, Rose also created Angelsoft (now Gust), a software company serving groups of angel investors, managing their organizations, their events, and information on investment opportunities. Angels and entrepreneurs have progressively been adoptingthe platform across the United States and around the world. As of December 2012, Gust was used in six languages and 195 countries by over 42,000 angel investors and 165,000 early stage companies, and had processed over $1.8 billion of startup investments. In 2012 it was named the most innovative financial technology company in the world by the SWIFT banking industry association."

Howard Morgan began his career as an investor well before co-founding the New York Angels. "My blog is called WayTooEarly.com, because I made my money investing too early or way too early," jokes Morgan, who has been following high-tech since the early 1970s, when he was teaching Decision Sciences and Computer Science at the University of Pennsylvania. His research was on interface technology and on the optimization of computer networks and for that he was also a consultant to corporations and government agencies on the use of the Internet in its early days. "I remember an article from the 1980s on the Philadelphia Inquirer, where the reporter wrote with great astonishment: 'Dr. Morgan even believes that one day executives will write their own emails!'" says Morgan. "But even those of us who correctly anticipated the explosion of the PC and the Internet could not imagine how big it would become. Nicholas Negroponte, the founder of the Media Lab at MIT, told me that during a meeting with some of the Internet pioneers in 1993 he asked how many computers they believed there would be in the year 2000. The highest number he was given was 30 million. In reality there were going to be 500 million."

Morgan is a real New Yorker. He was born in the Bronx in 1945 and earned his BS in Physics from City College in 1965. He then went to Cornell University for his doctorate in Operations Research. His father was a furrier. "Three years ago I experienced something wonderful," he remembers "I went to give a talk at a high-tech incubator on Ninth Avenue at the corner of 35th street, which was once at the center of the garment industry. Entering the building I immediately thought it looked familiar. And then I realized it was the same building where my dad had made fur sleeves and necks for 35 years. Now it has been completely redone as a high-tech building, rewired for high-speed communications and with better power, and connected to the Internet via fiber optics. All of a sudden, it's a high-tech building full of technology startups."

After ten years in academia, Morgan went into business: in 1981 he was a founding board member of Franklin Electronic Publishers, at first a PC manufacturer, and then a successful publisher of dictionaries and other content in electronic format (Morgan is still the Chairman of the company); from '82 to '89 he co-founded and managed, with James Simons, Renaissance Technologies, a fund that specialized in quantitative trading and technology venture capital, and that today is still one of the better known and best performing players in the hedge fund industry; and in 1990 he became an "angel." "I was pretty successful: in 1996, when the markets were bubbling, I took six companies public in six months, I re-invested the proceeds in Idealab, one of the first real high-tech incubators created by Bill

Gross in Pasadena, California," says Morgan. "Bill is a brilliant guy. He was the first one to patent paid search, so the whole model Google is based on was created at IdeaLab, and Google eventually paid $600 million dollars for the rights to continue using the algorithm. With Bill we decided to open IdeaLab New York in 1999, but when the market began to collapse in March 2000 we understood that it was the beginning of a tough period and we shut it down immediately."

Two of the startups Morgan successfully invested in as an angel were Infonautics (founded in 1992, then merged with Tucows in 2001 after going public) and Half.com (started in 1999 and purchased by eBay in 2000 for over $300 million): both were founded by Josh Kopelman, who ended up partnering with Morgan to launch a new venture capital firm at the end of 2004, First Round Capital, focused on startups, especially in New York. "Today we have over 50 New York companies in our portfolio, including Fab.com, a great success in the design and fashion industry," explains Morgan. "We usually are the most active venture firm in the city in number of new deals. We started to be more aggressive in 2005, when we saw New York starting to heat up. The turning point came with the sale of DoubleClick that year for $1.1 billion: exits like that are essential to grow the high-tech ecosystem, because the managers and engineers who have made some money selling their company can then take some risks and invest in other startups, created by them or by others."

"DoubleClick was a significant company for the growth of New York as a startup-friendly environment," confirms Fred Wilson. "A lot of talent came out of there. You could even call it the Hewlett-Packard of New York, reminiscent of the role HP had in making Silicon Valley flourish. Granted that the analogy does not work in many ways because HP dates back to 1939."

Many distinguished alumni have come out of DoubleClick to

pursue other entrepreneurial activities. CEO Ryan resigned after selling the company in 2005 to the San Francisco private equity firm of Hellman & Friedman, and is now head of Gilt Groupe. In 2007, when the private equity investors sold DoubleClick to Google for $3.1 billion, then CEO David Rosenblatt left to create Group Commerce. Also from DoubleClick are Mike Walrath, founder of Right Media (sold to Yahoo! for over 800 million dollars), and Bill Wise, who became CEO of MaxOnline and of other Internet companies.

Another encouraging sign for the establishment of New York as a technology hub was the decision by Google to open a large site in Chelsea in 2006, in a building that occupies an entire city block. Google has invested a great deal, hiring hundreds of engineers from a number of geographies, resulting in an increase of the talent pool in New York City.

That same year, Alan Patricof, the "grand old man" of venture capital in New York, decided to get back into the game by founding a new investment firm, Greycroft Partners. He was 71, with a record of substantial successes obtained with his first creature, Patricof & Co., established in 1969 and then grown, with other European partners, to become one of the largest private equity firms in the world: Apax (an acronym for "Alan Patricof Associates Cross Border"). In 1979, for example, he had been an early investor in Apple: "I'll be honest, a boutique investment firm, Unterberg Towbin, had offered us the deal. I quickly got what Apple was trying to accomplish and the technology approach it was using and realized the opportunity might move quickly away from us. Thus I took it on the fly, opportunistically, without doing any specific research, because it seemed to be such an exciting young company," says Patricof, speaking from his offices in the heart of Manhattan on Madison Avenue and 57th Street, where he continues to work full time with the same energy of 40 years ago. In 1982 it was the time of

AOL. "In that case I had gone to meet management in Washington, DC and they asked me to join their Board of Directors but I declined because we didn't have a significant enough position," he adds. In 2001 Patricof retired from the active management of Apax to rethink the whole business of venture capital.

"Many firms, including the one I built, had grown in size, doing only mega transactions, while on the other hand, the need for capital for startups was decreasing as a result of technology outsourcing, cloud computing and the reduction in the cost of components," recalls Patricof. "In short, there was a market opportunity and I thought I'd take advantage of that with a new kind of venture capital fund: small, with less than $200 million, focused on capital efficient businesses, aiming to exit not with an IPO but with an M&A transaction; and focused primarily on digital media." One of his most successful moves was his decision to participate in 2006-2007 in the first two rounds of financing of *The Huffington Post*, "the newspaper of the future," according to him, together with SoftBank Capital, Ken Lerer and Bob Pittman: around $10 million that yielded an excellent return, when the Arianna Huffington's site was sold to AOL for $315 million in 2011.

The Huffington Post is a perfect example of how Greycroft Partners works, says Patricof: "Co-investing with others, without a minimum threshold. We can go from a few hundred thousand dollars to $4 million. And own anywhere between 1% and 20% of the companies we invest in. We are flexible and that's why both entrepreneurs and co-investors like us. And our Limited Partners are happy because a series of investments we have made have returned between four and ten times their money." The biggest recently was Buddy Media: together with other VCs, Greycroft Partners had participated investing four million dollars out of a total of $30 million raised between 2008 and 2010: Salesforce.com acquired it for $689 million in cash and stock in June 2012, now worth a lot more thanks to the increase in the value of Salesforce's stock. Greycroft owned 10% of the company.

Buddy Media was the star celebrated on June 5, 2012 at the NY Tech Meetup. "NYTM was born as a logical follow-on to Meetup," explains its founder Heiferman, picking up the thread of his story started with September 11. "When Meetup was two years old, I was wondering why on earth there was no community of Internet people in NY. Many years before, when I was working at Sony in 1994, I met this guy named Kyle Shannon who decided to start what was then called the World Wide Web Artists Consortium (WWWAC), a monthly gathering of people who were interested in the Web. That was a grand total of 14 people for a while in New York City, but eventually it grew to 40 people and it was incredibly inspiring and valuable, in 1994 and 1995, to have this gathering and this community; even more so because I was the only person at Sony doing work on the web. Coincidentally then Kyle co-founded Agency.com, which in 1999 bought my startup i-Traffic. WWWAC disappeared around 1998. Flash forward to 2004 and I decided to form the NY Tech Meetup and convene the first meeting. One person showed up, Dawn Barber; the second month we were four; the third we were 14 and we have grown like that, gradually, organically." Up to today at the Skirball Center, with 850 people, the lucky ones who manage to grab tickets when they are offered online, going like hotcakes in minutes.

"At the first meeting I stood up and proclaimed: we are the New York high-tech community!" says Heiferman. "It felt weird when we were 20 or 40, also because I didn't even know what was a community. But you declare it and then it must be, and what is fascinating is to see how the New York Tech community really considers itself a community now. And even more interesting than the NYTM are 500 other tech-related Meetups in New York: there are some for each category of technology or application, from Java to Big Data. I am convinced that New York, thanks to this strong, dense network of communities, will become a great tech city in the future."

3
The Future Is .NYC
Bloomberg, the Financial Crisis and the Diversification of the NY Economy

"I was terminated from the only full-time job I'd ever known and from the high-pressure life I loved. This, after fifteen years of twelve-hour days and six-day weeks. Out!" This could have been the grumble of thousands of traders who lost their jobs after the collapse of Lehman Brothers, on September 15, 2008. A crash that marked the end of an era on Wall Street, exacting heavy losses on the economy of New York, and at the same time forcing the City to "re-invent" itself one more time.

Instead it was the 108th Mayor, Michael Bloomberg, telling firsthand what happened to him on August 1, 1981 in the chapter "The last supper: the thrill of getting fired" of his autobiography, *Bloomberg by Bloomberg*[1]. It was just at the beginning of the longest and most severe recession since WWII (from July '81 to November '82) prior to the one triggered by the subprime crisis. Not the ideal time to be fired.

But Bloomberg still talks about it as the lucky break of his career. "After all, losing a job can be a golden opportunity to start your own business. (Thank you very much, Salomon Brothers)," said the Mayor in his speech to the Economic Club of New York on March 23, 2009, at the height of the great recession (lasting from December 2007 to June 2009, according to official statistics of the National Bureau of Economic Research). He explained how his administration intended to overcome the crisis by encouraging the entrepreneurial spirit of the City, with many new initiatives to attract "the best and brightest" brains and help them build their startups.[2]

His dismissal was literally "golden": he was a partner at Salomon Brothers, one of the most important investment banks on Wall Street in the 1970s, and his severance was worth $10 million, an astronomical figure at the time. He used four of those millions to create his startup, Innovative Market Solutions, which in 1986 changed its name to Bloomberg L.P. Today it's an empire with 310,000 worldwide subscribers, on whose desks you can find the unmistakable terminals, indispensable tool for those working in the financial markets. A success that Bloomberg has built putting to good use his passion for technology and his love for risk; and that is critical to understanding his later politics, as Mayor, to relaunch New York as a new "Tech City."

A billionaire today—the 11th richest in the United States according to the most recent Forbes ranking,[3] with an estimated wealth of $22 billion—Bloomberg grew up in an ordinary family in Medford, near Boston, Massachusetts. His father worked seven days a week as a bookkeeper at a dairy. The values inherited by his parents are those of the "basic middle-class (…): the importance of hard work, of contributing to those less fortunate, of getting past adversity and not dwelling on setbacks," explained to *The New York Times*[4] Joyce Purnick, author of the biography *Mike Bloomberg: Money, Power, Politics.*[5]

From an early age he was fascinated by technology. "I grew up going to the Museum of Science in Boston, every Saturday morning," Bloomberg told NPR[6]. So he chose to major in electrical engineering at Johns Hopkins University, but then he also went to the Harvard Business School for his MBA and with that, in 1966, just 24-years of age, he began his career at Salomon Brothers. A humble beginning, starting at the lowest rung of the corporate hierarchy: for most of the first year he worked in the Bank's vault—without air conditioning, frequently working in his underwear to withstand the torrid heat—counting billions of dollars in stock and bond certificates to send to other banks as lending collateral.

But soon the young Bloomberg advanced, becoming first a trader, then promoted to chief of stock trading—a new business for Salomon, till then specialized in bonds—and finally a General Partner of the bank, at only 31 in 1973. Unlike his rival Richard Rosenthal, however, he was never part of the Executive Committee—the Group of partners with the final decision authority. And Rosenthal, by then part of the decision-making body, managed in 1979 to relegate Bloomberg to the "Siberia" of Technical Support, considered the least prestigious department at Salomon Brothers. Rather than getting discouraged and quitting, Bloomberg turned his demotion into an opportunity to prototype what would later become his winning product: the terminal that bears his own name.

Until then, traders did not have computers on their desks—they thought it was the stuff of secretaries or underpaid researchers—and in order to get prices or information on securities to be traded they would rely on Wall Street Journal listings, and then figure out trades using calculators. The company's major technological investment was in large IBM mainframes, locked in the "computer room." Bloomberg instead understood that the future was to make small machines directly accessible by traders, and able to respond quickly to their queries. And he started to provide his colleagues with a service he developed, the "B-pages," that not only provided pricing data on listed companies, but also calculated the impact on markets of any news such as changes in interest rates. No one at the top of Salomon Brothers had realized the importance of these innovations. So when the shakeup took place, Bloomberg was fired.

"I'd never have left voluntarily," Bloomberg wrote in his autobiography. "There'd be no reason to in good times, and I couldn't have abandoned them in bad times. Unfortunately (or fortunately for me, as it turned out), staying wasn't an option."[7] The weekend that changed his life started with a celebration on Friday, July 31: the Executive Committee of Salomon Brothers had summoned him and the other 62 partners to the Tarrytown Conference Center, outside New York, to announce the decision to sell the Bank to Phibro Corporation, a publicly-traded commodities firm. A big deal that suddenly made all the partners wealthy. But after an evening of debauchery—eating juicy steaks, drinking liquor, smoking cigars and playing poker—typical "vices" of those "roaring" Wall Street years, came the rude awakening. "Time for you to leave,"[8] John Gutfreund, the head of Salomon, told Bloomberg, sweetening the pill with a $10 million golden handshake. In the power struggle with Rosenthal, Bloomberg had clearly lost.

Saddened, but too "macho" to show it, the newly unemployed immediately started thinking of what to do the next day, without turning back. "Once finished: Gone. Life continues!" he recalled in his autobiography. His last day at Salomon was September 30, 1981. "Next morning I started Bloomberg, the company."[9]

It was the middle of a severe national recession. But Bloomberg was able to create his own computer firm, far away from Silicon Valley, because "New York had provided him with the critical requirements for entrepreneurship: skilled workers, financing, access to customers, and knowledge," noted the Harvard Economics Professor Edward Glaeser in the 2009 article *The Reinventive City*.[10] Even while the after-shocks of the Lehman collapse were still evident, Glaeser's thesis was that New York would overcome even the last recession and reinvent itself one more time, thanks to its strengths: "competition, diversity, access to the world, and, most of all, human capital, made even more potent through proximity."[11] New York is the quintessential big city that thrives connecting people and magnifies talents by concentrating them. And the way Bloomberg's offices are designed is a reflection of that concept and another reason for the company's success: all open space, with no physical barriers among its workers, to encourage people's proximity and constantly exchange information.

Bloomberg took the same "open office" model to City Hall when he became mayor in January 2002. He knocked down the dividers and opened up the main floor of the municipal administration's office, just like a large financial trading floor, so that dozens of managers and assistants are always accessible, ready to receive input and to account for their decisions. And he also brought along his management style, not "political" but focused on data analysis to solve practical problems.

Inaugurated Mayor while the rubble of the Twin Towers was still smoldering, at the end of his second term Bloomberg had to cope with another major shock to New York, the crash of Lehman. "Handling this financial crisis while strengthening essential services is a challenge I want to take on,"[12] he explained at a press conference two weeks after the collapse of the Wall Street bank, announcing that he would be a candidate for re-election in 2009 and asking to change the law limiting New York City mayors to two terms. The City Council supported him and New Yorkers gave him confidence, although with a reduced margin (50.7% of votes against 46.3% of his opponent, Bill Thompson, while four years earlier he had won with a gap of 20 percentage points).

A key objective of Bloomberg's third term was to diversify the city's economy, where the financial industry accounted for, until 2009, a third of total personal income in the private sector. In the two years since the outbreak of the financial crisis on Wall Street, banks had lost $54 billion dollars of market capitalization and a quarter of their employees: a hole that could not be filled only by tourism or from films shot in Manhattan, despite a rise in the latter.

Hence the push to re-launch New York as a new "Tech City," using in particular the professionalism of the New York City Economic Development Corporation (NYCEDC), the not-for-profit entity that reports directly to the Mayor's Office and is responsible for encouraging the economic development of the city. It is led by Seth Pinsky, a 40-year-old lawyer recruited in 2008 by then-Deputy Mayor for economic matters Daniel Doctoroff, who is now CEO of Bloomberg L.P.

With a reputation as a tough negotiator, gained throughout the lengthy discussions for the reconstruction of the World Trade Center, Pinsky brought into the NYCEDC a group of young professionals willing to work for a period of their lives serving the community. It is the team of the Center for Economic Transformation (CET), a bridge between Government and private entrepreneurs, especially those in the high-tech sector. They are the ones who, for example, organized a dozen incubators, from the Bronx to Brooklyn, which in three years gave birth to over 40 companies. These incubators are not managed directly by city structures, a CET manager emphasized. The direct approach was tried years ago and failed. With Bloomberg the philosophy is different. Civil servants are helping the various stakeholders collaborate: on the one hand, the building managers, and on the other the operators that want to manage an incubator; public money only facilitate the startup phase, while responsibility for the functioning of the incubator, and its profit and loss, is up to the private partners, which the CET continues to monitor as long as it is needed.

Visiting the offices of NYCEDC in 2012 you can feel a sense

of urgency: just a few months from the end of the Bloomberg administration, Pinsky and his team are intent on picking what priorities to focus on, aiming to finish as many projects as possible. No one can say it, but everyone is worried about the after-Bloomberg. "This Mayor is unique," says a CET team-member, who wants to remain anonymous. "He really understands technology, business, startups. It is for this reason that many talented people have agreed to come and work here. He wants us to act as entrepreneurs, taking risks without fear of failure. What will happen after him?"

The tech community in New York has the same fears. "I'm terrified thinking about the post Bloomberg," blurted out Lawrence Lenihan, founder and managing partner of the New York venture capital firm FirstMark Capital, one of the participants at the annual "Venture Forward" conference, produced by Gust, on June 20th, 2012. It was a crisp and sunny day and the view from the offices of the New York Academy of Sciences on the 40th floor of 7 World Trade Center, the first skyscraper rebuilt on Ground Zero and where the conference was taking place, was breathtaking.

Over 200 "angels" and other private investors were discussing the future of startups, a stone's throw from the construction site around Ground Zero: a constant reminder of the fragility and at the same time the strength of New York, and the generosity of those who work there and who, when successful, are ready to give back a portion of their fortune to the community.

"Give back to improve the world: it is a principle of Jewish ethics," says Brian Cohen, Chairman of the New York Angels since October 2011. "If you make money and you have more than you need, you have to figure out a way to improve the world. It's actually your job. It's your responsibility," explains

Cohen. "If you apply this principle, understand that being an angel also means doing good: help these young, bright entrepreneurs develop their ideas and, with them, grow the economy as a whole."

Born in Brooklyn, New York, 57 years ago, Cohen is one of the many entrepreneurs and investors of Jewish origin that animate the high-tech New York scene. "Like all Jewish boys of my generation I grew up wanting to become a doctor," joked Cohen. "But in college I realized that it wasn't my vocation and I discovered instead a passion for science and technology. So in 1976 I joined the first Master of Science and Technology Journalism program at Boston University, where I had the opportunity to follow the fledgling computer industry and get to know all its main characters."

Back in New York after getting his degree, in 1978 Cohen started a small but successful publication, *Computer Systems News*. "But journalism doesn't pay and in 1983 I created the first PR agency specialized in high-tech: Technology Solutions Inc. (TSI)," says Cohen. "All major technology groups became my clients, starting with IBM for which I created, among other things, the Deep Blue challenge to chess champion Kasparov—a big hit. TSI's business grew fast and financed itself. I loved my work so much that I named one of my kids Trace, the name of a supercomputer built by one of my clients, Multiflow. But in the spring of 1997, in the midst of irrational exuberance, I realized that hard times were coming and I decided to sell the company. I managed to sell it on July 3rd of that same year, earning millions of dollars. The next day I was with my wife Carol at Disneyworld."

Tied to a non-compete agreement for five years, Cohen decided to retire in 1999 on Long Island, build a house for his family and become a full-time dad to his three children, who were ten, seven and five at the time. "The best decision of my life," he recalls. "My wife and I dedicated ourselves to volunteering and charitable giving. But after a few years, with our kids off to school, we decided to return to the city. And I started to make angel investments."

His biggest hit so far is making the first investment in Pinterest, the popular social network used to share photos, organized as collections of pictures on a pin board. Launched in March 2010, it has become one of the most visited sites, with 23 million users in 2012 and a valuation of over $1.5 billion. Pinterest was founded in Palo Alto, Silicon Valley, by three youngsters under 30. "I helped them start and guided them as a mentor to become what they are," says Cohen. "With this single investment I'm done. As soon as I get my liquidity event I will party like there's no tomorrow."

All the angels dream of "the big hit," says Cohen, who has written a book on the subject.[13] They are the ones providing 90% of startup capital, by writing checks out of their own pocket. But they don't do it just thinking of financial returns. "I think we do it because it's fun. There's no question that everyone thinks he or she is smarter than everyone else," the Chairman of the New York Angels says half-jokingly. "In reality no one makes money, although some are luckier and hit the jackpot. Then there is the fashion factor. Everyone today wants to be an angel because it is cool. In other words, we are the prima donnas; we have a big ego. But there is also the idea of doing good, to have the satisfaction of helping start new emerging companies." The pleasure of giving back: an important part of Jewish culture, and of American culture in general.

"Give back" is the philosophy that for over 30 years inspired Charles Francis Feeney, an Irish-American born in 1931 in Elizabeth, New Jersey, a self-made billionaire for having invented "duty free shopping," and built the DFS chain of stores around the world. It is thanks to him and to his contribution of

THE FUTURE IS .NYC

$350 million that the new campus of Cornell NYC Tech is going to be built in the city of New York. This is the new Institute of higher learning (postgraduate) resulting from the joint venture between Cornell University and the Technion-Israel Institute of Technology: its goal is to promote innovation and create high-tech entrepreneurship, jobs and economic growth in the city.[14]

"Chuck" Feeney had studied at the Cornell University School of Hotel Administration and over the years has given hundreds of millions of dollars to his Alma Mater, remaining anonymous for a long time, so that no plaque bears his name on the campus in Ithaca, 220 miles north-west of New York City. Of humble origins, Feeney had begun to make money by selling duty-free liquor crates to U.S. Navy personnel in ports of the Mediterranean in the 1950s. In 1960, along with partner Robert Miller, he founded DFS in Hong Kong, and eventually sold it to French conglomerate LVMH for $1.6 billion in 1996. Already in 1982, though, Feeney had created The Atlantic Philanthropies, a charitable foundation that is managing much of his heritage, $9 billion, with the commitment of giving it away completely by 2017. "I had one idea that never changed in my mind—that you should use your wealth to help people. I try to live a normal life, the way I grew up. I set out to work hard, not to get rich," explained Feeney to Conor O' Clery, author of his biography.[15]

"Give back" was also the reason why Greg Pass decided to leave San Francisco and come to New York. "One of the unsung heroes of the Twitter success story,"[16] says venture capitalist Fred Wilson, who knows him well, having invested in Twitter since the early days. Pass is the Chief Entrepreneurial Officer of Cornell NYC Tech: responsible for the merger of academic programs and "apprenticeship" that is going to be a feature of the entrepreneurial campus. He's only 36 years old, but he has a lot of experience in the field of startups. His first company was conceived while studying computer science, with a specialization in cognitive studies, at Cornell. Working from 1995 to 1997 in the Robotics Laboratory at the University, Pass developed a technology for finding images on the Internet that became the core of ToFish, founded in 1998 and sold to AOL in January 2000. After six years with AOL as a systems architect and software engineer, Pass went back on his own in 2007 with Summize, a real-time search engine, that Twitter bought in July 2008.

"At that time Twitter was experiencing very difficult scaling problems. The service was down a lot and was slow when it was up," recalled Wilson on his blog.[17] "It has come a very long way in less than two years. (…) Twitter has grown by 50x in that time and has increased its reliability and scalability dramatically. And the Summize engineering team had a lot to do with that. Greg Pass, who was Summize's co-founder and VP Engineering, became Twitter's engineering leader in the summer of 2008 and has built the team from roughly a dozen to somewhere around ten times that number. (…) He brought a calm, steady hand to a ship that was caught in a storm. He got it going in the right direction and headed for calmer waters." Pass remained at Twitter as Chief Technology Officer until the summer of 2011, when he agreed to engage in the Cornell NYC Tech project.

"I've been fortunate to have had some success as an entrepreneur and I think it's important, when opportunities come up, to give back to that profession in some way," said Pass to *Business Insider*[18] explaining why he chose to leave Twitter for Cornell NYC Tech. Selling him on this new mission was Dan Huttenlocher, the Dean of Computing and Information Science at Cornell, who has known him for a long time and is now the Dean of the new campus.

"Cornell NYC Tech is one of the best things Mayor Bloomberg has done. It will have a huge long-term impact," said Kevin Ryan, the most admired entrepreneur in the New York high-tech community. Cornell's President David Skorton is certain that the new Institute will make New York "the new technology capital of the world." And Bloomberg has called this project, which will cost around two billion dollars and will be completed in 2037, "transformative."[19]

The construction of the campus on Roosevelt Island, a strip of land on the East River between Manhattan and Queens, will create 20,000 construction jobs and then up to 8,000 permanent jobs, according to estimates by the city administration; and the campus is expected to generate nearly 600 startups in the coming 30 years, generating another 30,000 jobs and $1.4 billion dollars in tax revenues for New York.[20] The city "gives away" the land—11 acres on the Island South of the Queensboro Bridge, now occupied by an old hospital—and an investment of $100 million dollars in infrastructure improvements. The rest is entirely self-financed.

It is a huge project that Bloomberg hopes will become the most prestigious legacy of his administration. Ambition, of course, is one of his drivers. But there's also his desire of not being known only for his wealth, but for having made a real difference. The same desire that led him to become an Eagle Scout, the highest award of the Boy Scouts of America, for special achievements, as Purnick explained in her biography of Bloomberg.[21]

The idea took shape in the midst of recession after the Lehman collapse, while the need to diversify the economy of New York beyond Wall Street was becoming crystal-clear. A promising sector was high-tech, with a series of growing startups—Gilt Groupe, Etsy, Tumblr, Foursquare—struggling to find enough engineers and other qualified staff. "The city leaders—everybody from the Mayor to the business elite—have all concluded that New York is not focused enough on technology education and that the big educational institutions are not connected enough to the startup world," notes Fred Wilson.

The comparison that immediately comes to mind is with Stanford, which played a key role in the development of Silicon Valley. But another model of virtuous relationship between technology business and academics comes from the Technion, Israel's oldest University (whose construction started in 1912, with studies beginning in 1924), often referred to as the MIT of Israel: 70% of its graduates in applied sciences—from core engineering disciplines to industrial management—work in the high-tech sector; and half of the 121 Israeli company traded on the NASDAQ stock exchange are led by alumni of the Technion. It is discussed in the best-selling 2009 book *Startup Nation*[22] that immediately became "the book" to read at City Hall, among the Mayor's staff, according to *Newsweek Magazine*.[23]

So Technion was one of the Universities contacted in early 2010 by the New York City Economic Development Corporation to probe whether they would be interested in creating a new institute of applied sciences in New York. The official "Request for Proposal" was launched in December 2010. Twenty proposals were submitted by the summer of 2011, including that of Stanford, which eventually retired from the "race" without specifying why. A possible reason is that the California institute realized at some point that the alliance between Cornell and Technion would have been unbeatable. The first, a New York State Ivy League institution with great competence in technical disciplines: Computer Science, Electrical and Computer Engineering, Materials Science and Nanotechnology, and Information Science; the second, closely linked to the business world and to the Jewish community of the Big Apple. In fact David S. Rose's family provided the funding that supported Technion's side of the joint venture with Cornell.

The announcement of the winning pair was made December 19,

2011. "Today will be remembered as a defining moment," said Bloomberg solemnly, explaining that he had chosen the project of Cornell-Technion because it was "far and away the boldest and most ambitious" and had "an incredibly aggressive schedule"[24] for its implementation. First stage: the establishment of a pilot class in January 2013, into a space offered free by Google in its mega-building in Chelsea, with a class of 20 students selected not only on the basis of their academic credentials, but also for their potential as "future tech leaders," with "strong entrepreneurial interests, leadership skills and a passion for community engagement," said Dean Huttenlocher. This first class—"beta" as a high-tech prototype—lasts two semesters and confers a Cornell Master of Engineering degree in Computer Science: to achieve this, students must complete "a substantial project co-supervised by a faculty member and an industry mentor, with a written report rather than a formal research thesis."[25]

Meanwhile Huttenlocher along with Pass and the other two executives of Cornell NYC Tech—vice president Cathy Dove (former associate dean in the College of Engineering at Cornell) and the founding director Craig Gotsman, professor of Computer Science at the Technion—must develop the curriculum of an innovative two-year Master of Science degree that will be at the heart of the new campus. The interdisciplinary approach will be organized around three "hubs": "Connective Media" (technologies applicable to digital media but also to other businesses such as finance); "Healthier Life" (health sector) and "Built Environment" (architecture and sustainable development); but the focus will change and grow along the trends of the technology industry.

The courses will continue to be hosted by Google until 2017, when the first building on the Roosevelt Island campus will be inaugurated. The construction is scheduled to begin in 2014, after the current hospital is emptied (by transferring patients to other facilities) and demolished. Fully implemented, the campus will have over 200 faculty and 2000 students, each with an "industry" mentor. "It will be something more akin to an apprenticeship," explains Pass. "You're sourced with an industry advisor who's literally invested in your success and paying attention to your success ... Cornell Tech is somewhere in between academia and industry experience, a lot of the things that would happen at Y Combinator ... would be part of this program."[26]

"Ten years from now, we'll see a boy from Georgia, who wants to get his Master's degree in computer science, getting into Cornell-Technion. He's happy because it's a good school," says Ryan. "And when he graduates, he'll end up staying in New York for a variety of reasons: he's already here, his girlfriend wants to stay ... What does he do? He'll work for 10gen for three years, then go off, start his own company and create 3,000 jobs. All of that happened thanks to the Cornell campus here in NYC. If he had gone to Stanford, he would have done it in San Francisco. There'll be a lot of that happening: I think there will be tens of thousands of jobs directly or indirectly created just because there's a campus here."

It is the bet of New York City Tech. Ten years from now we will be able to gauge its accomplishments. Silicon Valley has become what it is over the course of decades: Stanford was founded in 1891 and Hewlett-Packard, the "mother of all startups," in 1939.

But the Big Apple has already beaten the California rival on at least one thing: it is the first city in the United States to be awarded its own top-level Internet domain (TLD).[27]

The new domain is ".nyc," conquered in the summer of 2012 by the City. The administration manages it and plans, starting in 2013, to allow its use first for public and not-for-profit institutions, then for residents and local businesses, and finally for organizations that offer specific services to New York.

"With the historic launch of the .nyc TLD, the City will embrace its digital future in a powerful way and bring an unprecedented level of geographic authority to the digital sphere. In addition, the City will generate revenue, help residents locate government services, encourage local businesses to thrive, market and promote tourism, and spread the dynamic image of New York City around the world," reads the Bloomberg Administration's Digital Roadmap of August 2012.[28]

And who knows, 2013 could also be the year in which the early graduates of Cornell NYC Tech create the first ".nyc" startup that will change, for the better, our life more than Facebook or Apple did.

II

Geography

A Stroll around New York's Startup Neighborhoods

4

The Heart of Silicon Alley

Flatiron and Union Square

Eataly has become the third most popular tourist attraction in New York after the Empire State Building and the Metropolitan Museum of Art. But legions of gourmets and curious visitors usually are unaware that this mecca of "Made in Italy" delights is located in the historic heart of Silicon Alley. Eataly is in the shadow of the Flatiron Building, one of the oldest skyscrapers in the city, and also a symbol of the first generation of Manhattan dot-coms in the '90s. The building's unmistakable triangular shape dominated the cover of the special November 13, 1995 issue of *New York* Magazine: "High-Tech Boom Town."[1] In that same year, Fred Wilson was to choose Flatiron as the name of his new venture capital firm specializing in the Internet. Next to the Flatiron Building, high up on Broadway at 22nd street, one of the successful startups of those years would install a huge billboard to herald the urban version of Silicon Valley: "DoubleClick welcomes you to Silicon Alley."[2]

More than ten years after the burst of the Internet bubble, the Flatiron District is still the area with the highest concentration of Internet investors and startups. But they no longer advertise themselves on billboards. Instead, they prefer a low profile—a hard learned lesson from a season of excess.

Another two blocks down, on Broadway between 20th and

21st streets, you can find the headquarters of Wilson's new venture capital firm, Union Square Ventures (USV). This time, the name is in honor of the area that has become the new center of activities for the startup community. Nearby at 40 Irving Place, is the Academy For Software Engineering (AFSE), a school for innovative teaching of computer science to students of secondary schools that opened in September 2012. On the same stretch of Broadway is General Assembly, the largest "campus" for New York startups. Farther west on 21st Street are the offices of Hunch's founder, Chris Dixon, the number one high-tech angel investor in America according to *Bloomberg BusinessWeek*. And Tumblr, one of the most successful and fastest growing among the new social media startups, is a bit farther east.

Four blocks south, at the corner of Park Avenue South and Union Square, is another important venture capital firm, First Round Capital. Founded by Josh Kopelman and Howard Morgan, First Round was in 2011 the most active firm in New York by number of investments.[3] Kevin Ryan, the CEO responsible for DoubleClick's growth from 1996 until 2005, when he sold it for over $1 billion, chose a stretch of Park Avenue a bit farther north, between 32nd and 33rd streets as headquarters of his new creation, Gilt Groupe. Two of Ryan's many admirers, Rohan Deuskar and Zach Davis, have set up Stylitics nearby.

To be accurate, Flatiron Partners did not have an office in the landmark skyscraper itself, but on Park Avenue and 21st Street, just steps from the current offices of USV. Wilson and his co-founder, Jerry Colonna, had chosen the building's name and silhouette as their symbol because they were "evocative of New York but kind of insidery," and therefore captivating to the mid-'90s tech community that was flourishing in the neighborhood. Newmark & Co., the Flatiron building's manager, ended up suing Flatiron Partners for infringement, claiming trademark rights for the image of the building. At the end of 1999, at the peak of the dot-com boom, the venture firm had to pay to continue using its logo.[4]

Today the Flatiron building is still a symbol of those roaring '90s, when, as Wilson recalls today, "there was this gold rush mentality, and everybody jumped in." But the original premise that inspired the founding of Flatiron Partners proved sound, "that the Internet would be big and that New York City would be an important locus of Internet innovation," according to Wilson's blog, AVC. "We did not invest in DoubleClick, sadly, but we did invest in a lot of interesting Internet companies in NYC in the late '90s," added Wilson.[5] In 1999 Yahoo! bought one of Flatiron's most famous startups, Geocities, for $3.5 billion: a major deal for Wilson who, ten years later, posted on his blog: "I learned that you can make 100 times your investment every once in a while. And when you do, it's something special."[6]

Born in 1961 at West Point, where his father, a career army officer, was a professor, Wilson was passionate about technology from an early age. As a boy, he had free access to the computer labs of the academy. His developing passion led him to study engineering at the Massachusetts Institute of Technology. There he met his wife, Joanne Solomon, whom Wilson married in 1987 and whose handle, "Gotham Gal" has become famous through her own tech blog. After earning an MBA from Wharton, Wilson began as an associate at Euclid Partners, an old line venture capital firm in the heart of Manhattan at Rockefeller Center. "My wife, who was born in Los Angeles, had her sights on New York as the most interesting place to live in the United States—that's why she decided to raise our family here," says Wilson, "and since then we have always been happy here, because the social life is so diverse. We've always been nervous about moving to California because we thought everything would be one-dimensional: everyone would be from the technology business."

After Flatiron Partners, which lasted from 1996 until the summer of 2000 when the fund ceased to invest and was eventually liquidated, Wilson founded USV in 2003 with Brad Burnham, a former general partner of AT&T Ventures. USV's focus is on technology-based services that can fundamentally transform industries by creating networks of "engaged" users. The portfolio holds the cream of New York startups: from 10gen to Etsy, from Foursquare to Kickstarter and Tumblr, in addition to a few Silicon Valley high-flyers such as Twitter and Zynga, purchased early in the life of USV.

From the windows of USV's offices, you can almost see the Washington Irving Educational Complex, where the Academy for Software Engineering (AFSE) opened its doors in the fall of 2012. According to its website, the school is for "the next generation of young people who dare to dream that anything is possible through software, design, technology and the human spirit." "It was my idea and I convinced the Department of Education to do it," says Wilson. "They did not know how to get it off the ground, so I donated and raised some money to help with the startup aspects of it."

The AFSE is not a specialized school, but in addition to the regular high school curriculum it teaches software programming, so that at the end of four years students can start working right away if they decide not to go to college. It's one of the many projects that Mayor Bloomberg's administration has undertaken to alleviate the shortage of a skilled high-tech labor force. And it receives support from many industry leaders with an established presence in New York, including Google, eBay, Facebook and Foursquare—companies that responded to Wilson's appeal for financial support. In addition, the corporate sponsors also helped in conducting the search for a Principal

(Seung Yu, with experience in another experimental school, the Pathways in Technology Early College High School in Brooklyn); in providing mentors for students; and by offering internships. If successful, this model could expand to other high schools in the city during the next few years.

The 20,000 square foot space of General Assembly (GA) looks like a university campus. "People always try to put us in a bucket. Oh, this is an incubator; this is a co-working space; this is a school... the reality is it's a mix of those things," insists Adam Pritzker, co-founder of GA and the one responsible for the architecture of its interiors. He did not study architecture: he learned a bit practicing it—according to the philosophy of General Assembly itself. A bit of it is in his DNA, being a heir to the family that founded and still controls the Hyatt hotel chain. "My hero and mentor was my grandfather," Adam says referring to his late grandfather Jay Pritzker who died in 1999.

"One story I like to tell about him is that, when he started, he was looking at a hotel in Atlanta that had a tall atrium that looked like a doughnut. When other big hotel chains looked at the property, they said 'fill this hole with rooms, and we'll start thinking about buying it.' But he thought that maybe a consumer would really love being in a beautiful, interesting architectural environment, and he ended up putting glass elevators in the atrium... hence he created a feature of Hyatt Hotels, an experience that even today leaves kids and adults open-mouthed in amazement, the first time they come."

Born and raised in San Francisco, Pritzker is 28 years old and has been living in New York since attending Columbia University, where he graduated with a degree in anthropology in 2007, subsequently working for a year and a half as an assistant to Jeffrey Sachs at the Earth Institute, where he focused on technology transfer in an effort to create businesses from intellectual property developed by the University. "The reality is that the capital expenditures required in Clean Technology are so incredibly high," says Pritzker, "that I didn't feel that I could do anything to make an impact, so I became interested in digital media, and established General Assembly in January 2010, along with Jake Schwartz, Brad Hargreaves and Matthew Brimer."

In less than two years GA had to double its space. In June 2012, they opened a second office in a nearby building. Since then, GA's courses been attended by 15,000 students, the school has 70 full-time employees in New York, and it has begun to export its formula abroad—first to London and Berlin—with the ambitious goal of creating a global network of campuses "for technology, business and design." In each location, Pritzker and his associates seek cooperation from the municipal administration, "because the projects need to be understood and supported also by the local authorities in a public-private partnership." In fact, the New York launch was awarded a $200,000 grant from Mayor Bloomberg.

"The humanistic education that we get in our universities teaches people to think critically and creatively, but it does not provide the skills to thrive in the work force in the 21st century," continues Pritzker. "It's also true that the college experience is valuable. The majority of your learning does not happen in the classroom. It happens in your dorm room or at dinner with friends. Even geniuses such as Mark Zuckerberg or Bill Gates, who both left Harvard to start their companies, came up with their ideas and met their co-founders in college."

Just as a college campus, GA has classrooms, whiteboard walls, a library, open spaces for casual meetings and discussions, bicycle parking, and lockers for personal belongings. But the emphasis is on "learning by doing" and gaining knowledge from those who are already working. Lectures can run the gamut from a single evening to a 16-week course, on subjects covering every conceivable matter relevant to technology startups— from how to create a web site to how to draw a logo, from seeking funding to hiring employees. But adjacent to the lecture halls, there is an area that hosts about 30 active startups in their infancy. "This is the core of our community," says Pritzker, showing the open space that houses the startups. "Statistically, not all of these companies are going to do well. I do believe, though, that all these people will. The cost of building technology is dropping so low that people can actually afford to take the risk to learn by doing something that, in our minds, is a much more effective way to learn than anything else. It's entrepreneurs who are in the field, learning by doing, putting journey before destination."

"Studying and working side by side is important, because from the interaction among people and the exchange of ideas, even informal, you learn, and other ideas are born," Pritzker emphasizes: "The Internet has not rendered in-person meetings obsolete and useless. We chose these offices just to be easily accessible by all—close to Union Square where almost every subway line stops—in particular those coming from Brooklyn, where many of our students live."

One of the most popular GA "professors" is Chris Dixon, a 40-year old regarded as the number one angel tech investor in America. He arrived in New York from his native Springfield, Ohio in order to attend Columbia, where he graduated with a B.A. and an M.A. in Philosophy. "Like a lot of people in this industry, I got a computer when I was nine. I've been programming since then. Then I went to college. The area of philosophy that I studied, logic and philosophy of mind, had a lot of crossovers with artificial intelligence, a topic I was interested in from computers," says Dixon at the offices of Hunch, the latest company he founded, and sold to eBay in 2011. At the entrance to his office on 21st Street, between Fifth and Sixth Avenues, there is an arcade video game machine. In the living room where Dixon holds his meetings, along with an electric guitar there's a stack of board games, including Monopoly, reflecting the playful side of the philosopher-entrepreneur. "While in college I was a programmer, working for a law firm and a hedge fund, which then offered me a job," continues Dixon. "I took the full-time job they offered me in order to pay off my student loans, but I left in '98. I did not like the yelling and the Wall Street culture. I worked for a couple of different Internet companies as a programmer, and I became interested in startups and venture capital. I wanted to enter that world, but I realized that I could only get jobs as a programmer. So, I applied to the Harvard Business School and got in. I remember reading all these business books like *Barbarians at the Gate*, *Liar's Poker*, and thinking 'what the hell is this?' I enjoyed it. Business school was interesting. I learned a lot of stuff."

Dixon got his first job in venture capital in 2003 at Bessemer Venture Partners. "Those were hard times for the industry and I was lucky to have this opportunity," says Dixon. "At first, though, I was involved with companies that were shutting down. I was thinking 'this is a terrible business!' But then I got involved with Skype, at the time an early-round investment, and I realized: 'OK, this is why people do this business.'"

But Dixon knew that getting a promotion would be tough because with ten associates and seven partners, the likelihood of becoming a partner in a reasonable timeframe was slim. He also had a strong desire to create his own startup. He looked for and found two MIT engineers as co-founders, and in 2005 launched SiteAdvisor, a service for monitoring the safety of websites. "We got several acquisition offers, and in the end we agreed to sell to McAfee in April 2006. So here my story splits in two: I remained an entrepreneur and started angel investing," says Dixon.

According to market estimates McAfee paid $70 million for SiteAdvisor. Between then and now, Dixon has reinvested his stake in forty startup companies as an angel investor. His investments include Foursquare, Kickstarter, Stripe, Dropbox and OMGPOP (bought by Zynga). He also invests through Founder Collective, a group of half a dozen venture capitalists and entrepreneurs formed in 2008. The group includes Scott Heiferman of MeetUp, and Caterina Fake, co-founder of Hunch. "Here at Hunch," adds Dixon, "there's also one of the co-founders of SiteAdvisor, Tom Pinckney, along with two other MIT engineers who worked in my first startup. At that time they had remained in Boston to take care of the technology while I was in New York for business. But we made a pact, that if we founded another company we would all work in New York. The promise was kept with Hunch."[7]

A New Yorker by birth is David Karp, the child prodigy who at age 21, in 2007, founded Tumblr, whose headquarters are located just one block east of Hunch. The son of a composer and a science teacher, at 14 Karp began working as an intern in an online animation company; at 15, tired of traditional school, he continued to study at home alone, learning, among other things, Japanese; then he became the chief technology officer of the Internet site UrbanBaby and at 17 he went to Tokyo for five months by himself. In 2006, CNET bought UrbanBaby, and Karp used his share of proceeds to establish Tumblr, a blogging platform with elements of social networking that allows its users to follow other bloggers. Tumblr allows users to build a collection of content according to their own tastes and interests.

Easy to use, with a format of short entries to be enriched with photos and videos, Tumblr has quickly gained many followers among the creative community as well as the public at large. Today it is home to nearly 70 million blogs, including those of Lady Gaga and Barack Obama, with a total audience of 140 million users. At 26, Karp is leading a company with over 100 employees, valued at more than $800 million, with shareholders of the caliber of Virgin Group's Richard Branson. He defines Tumblr as new media, as opposed to technology, and seeks to attract non-traditional ads, inviting brands to create awareness and desire in their ads, rather than just trying to capture intent. Karp has already received several acquisition offers from other media groups, but he has always refused because he thinks big: he wants to reach billions, not millions of users and one day be in a position to acquire rather than be acquired. Meanwhile, in order to grow he is convinced that New York City, the capital of media and advertising, is the right city.[8]

An entrepreneur who has already created not one, but two billion-dollar companies is Kevin Ryan, 48, former CEO of DoubleClick, the technology leader in Internet display advertising. Now Ryan heads Gilt Groupe and two other promising startups, Business Insider, and 10gen. Each of these companies have little in common, apart from their founders— Ryan and his technology right arm, Dwight Merriman—and the year they began, 2007, two years after the sale of DoubleClick and a year after the sale of their other two "inventions," ShopWiki and Panther Express.

"Dwight and I were arguably the world's experts in ad serving, and we could do more business in that area, but we were too bored," admits Ryan. "Instead we were just intellectually interested and challenged by doing things like launching a newspaper (*Business Insider*), launching a fashion company (Gilt Groupe), launching a database company (10gen). It was great fun, although I do not recommend it to anyone."

Enjoying work as well as free time, while always looking for new experiences to stimulate one's imagination—this is the common theme of Ryan's life. In this sense, Ryan is the paradigm of the New York entrepreneur, not monomaniacal about technology as many of his Silicon Valley peers. Ryan's youthful travel between America and Europe, his cosmopolitan culture, helped shape such a mentality. "Between five and seven I lived in Rome, then in Geneva up to when I was 13, always because of my father, who worked for Caterpillar," remembers Ryan. "It is thanks to having learned how to play soccer in Italy, as a child with my friends, every day on the street, that I was then accepted to Yale University. In Italy I was nothing special, but in the States I was better than all the other kids and that is why they recruited me." While attending Yale Ryan studied for a semester in Paris; then went on to work on Wall Street for an investment bank that sent him to London to cover French companies. Next he decided to get an MBA at INSEAD in Fontainebleau, France, where he remained to work for Disney for a couple of years. Back in New York in '94, he was ready to experience the first Internet boom.

His time in Europe led him to found Gilt Groupe. "I knew about Vente Privée, the French company selling branded products online at discounted prices, for members only and limited in time. Successful in France, it had yet to be imported to the U.S. After three weeks of reflection, I concluded that there was no good reason not to do it here and I decided to create Gilt Groupe." This insight is now worth one billion dollars, according to market estimates, with $600 million in revenue, 800 employees including 100 around the world, and 700 in New York offices that occupy two floors at 2 Park Avenue. On the lower floor there are two ping-pong tables, another sport Ryan loves, along with the bike he uses every year to climb the legendary Mont Ventoux in Provence.

The second company of his portfolio, Business Insider, is a site for news and commentary on economics and technology. With over 18 million unique visitors per month, it reaches more readers than the *Financial Times* and *Bloomberg BusinessWeek*. "The secret of its success is to give views that are intelligent and thought-provoking, give real substance with, at the same time, a much punchier presentation," says Ryan, defending the choice of Henry Blodget as its director, despite his past as a disgraced dot-com era financial analyst. "Henry has had trouble because he paradoxically complained about what was going on. He is the best writer out there. He's just remarkably talented—a lot of our success is really due to him and to how good he is."

And finally there is 10gen: "It is a core technology for the management of databases. It is used by about 40% of the startups in New York, plus the Wall Street Journal, AOL, eBay, and many other companies." Mayor Bloomberg, always careful to recognize the technology startups able to boost the city's economy, has visited their headquarters in NoLita more than once.[9]

"Gilt Groupe is an example of success we look to with admiration and a desire to emulate," add 30-year-old Rohan Deuskar and Zach Davis, founders of Stylitics, a company that analyzes fashion trends and has the potential, according to them, to be worth $1 billion just like Gilt Groupe. The two had met in Chicago in 2004: Deuskar, born in Mumbai, attended Northwestern University. Davis, a native of Iowa who has always been interested in sports and music, went to work for a digital music company. They originally met at a "cool" Chicago startup specialized in digital marketing, Vibes Media, where they became friends and dreamed of creating their own company. To understand how to do that, Deuskar decided to enroll at the Wharton School in 2009, where the project began to materialize, culminating with a victory at the school's Business Plan Competition.

Thus Stylitics was born between the fall of 2010 and the spring of 2011. In June of that year, they made the jump to New York. "We knew from the beginning that we would eventually move here, because this is the capital of fashion, media and advertising, all relevant sectors to Stylitics," Deuskar recalls. "We started with $90,000, a combination of my savings and the money won at the Wharton competition. It has not been easy to find space, recruit our first programmers, get known by investors. The first year we worked on a table in my apartment in Brooklyn, but now we have real Manhattan offices and we are close to all our partners" that already include famous brands such as Ralph Lauren and Forever21. For them Stylitics wants to be something like a Nielsen rating for consumer tastes in fashion: "Our aim is to capture real people behavior and we do it with the 'virtual wardrobe' of our website, where users can share with friends their style choices, shop and learn how to dress better. From there, we collect all the data anonymously, and we share it with brands and retailers. It is an analytical tool that tomorrow we can extend to other genres, and in fact we have already been contacted by a champagne producer." The Stylitics logo has already appeared on the Nasdaq screen in Times Square on August 23, 2011, to celebrate their win at the Wharton Business Plan Competition. Next time, Deuskar and Davis hope, it will be for a billionaire IPO.[10]

5
Tech and the City
The Meatpacking District and Chelsea

If "Sex and the City" were remade today, Carrie would fall in love with the founder of a technology startup and not with "Mr. Big." And the scenes filmed in the Meatpacking District—the area of New York where Carrie and her friends go shopping and have fun—would have a lot of close-ups of the new protagonists of this strip of the Big Apple that runs from Gansevoort Street on its southern border, to 16th Street on its northern one and from the Hudson river to the west, to Hudson Street and 8th or 9th Avenue to the east.

The new stars are the young people working in the hundreds of high-tech companies that decided to settle in this area. Until the 1990s, the area was strictly industrial with 250 butchers, slaughterhouses and meatpacking plants. Then, the transformation into the "most fashionable neighborhood"[1] of Manhattan began, with its boom of high-end boutiques, trendy restaurants and exclusive clubs. Today, the lofts that were carved out of the "historic" buildings no longer play host to the sexual prowess of Samantha, the least inhibited of the four single women in the famous TV series; instead they have become the headquarters of the latest startup wave. There are dozens of companies, for example, in the co-working spaces of WeWork, in a totally renovated building on Little West 12th.

The French bistro Bagatelle, famous for its wild "champagne brunch," is on the ground floor, while on the 5th floor you find the offices of the New York Angels, and on the 6th, Launch.it. "Today everyone, the kids and the not so young, is creating a startup to get laid on a Friday night," jokes Brian Cohen, chairman of the NY Angels and the founder of Launch.it.[2]

"The extraordinary thing is that nerds are cool today, and working at a startup is sexy," confirms Josh Miller, 22 years old. He is co-founder of Branch, a "platform for chatting online as if you were sitting around the table after dinner." Miller works at Betaworks, a hybrid company encapsulating a co-working space, an incubator and a venture capital fund, headquartered on 13th Street in the heart of the Meatpacking District. This kid in T-shirt and Bermuda shorts, and a potential star of the 2.0 version of Sex and the City, is super-excited by his new life as a digital neo-entrepreneur. He dropped out of Princeton in the summer of 2011 a year before getting his degree—heresy for the almost 30,000 students who annually apply to the prestigious Ivy League school in the hope of being among the 9% of applicants accepted.

What made him decide to take such a big step? An internship in the summer of 2011 at Meetup, the community site for those who organize meetings in the flesh for like-minded people. His leader, Scott Heiferman, took him to one of the monthly meetings of New York Tech Meetup and it was there that Miller saw the light. "It was the coolest thing that ever happened to me," he remembers. "All those people with such incredible energy. It was nothing like the sheltered atmosphere of Princeton." The next step was to take part in a seminar on startups where the idea for Branch came to him. He found two partners –students at NYU who could design a website. Heartened by having won a contest for Internet projects, Miller dropped out of Princeton.

"My parents told me I was crazy but I think they understood because they had also made unconventional choices when they were kids," says Miller. "My father, who is now a lawyer, played drums when he was at college, and he and my mother, who left home at 16, traveled around Europe for a year. I want to be a part of the new creative class that is pushing the boundaries farther. I want to contribute to making online discussion important again. Today there is nothing but the soliloquy of bloggers or rude anonymous comments."

The idea, something like a public group email exchange where one can contribute by invitation only, interested Twitter cofounder Biz Stone and other California investors who invited Miller and his team to move to San Francisco, financing them with a two million dollar investment. After only four months in California, Branch returned to New York, where it now employs a dozen or so people. "San Francisco was beautiful and I learned a lot from Biz and my other mentors, but there's much more adrenaline here," explains Miller, who is from California, born and raised in Santa Monica. "Life is more varied here and creating a technological startup is something new, unlike in San Francisco or Silicon Valley where everyone's doing it: it grabs you like a drug. Besides New York is the media capital and we're an online publishing organization so it's only right to be here."[3]

"What are we? Not an incubator. We work more as a fashion design studio," says John Borthwick, the 47-year-old founder and CEO of Betaworks. "We start out with an idea and quickly test it to see whether it responds to the needs of the public. If we get a positive result, we add other resources. If not, we drop the idea. But sometimes we invest in a product from the outside like Branch." TechCrunch defined Borthwick as "one of the most influential social web architects." He explains that he wants to contribute to the "reinvention" of media: "We are still at the beginning of this process. When a new technology is adopted there are always a number of companies that spring up. Just think of the hundreds of companies making cars in the U.S. at the beginning of the 20th century. Then comes consolidation and the new technology starts earning good money. Some media executives complain that 'an analog dollar has become a digital dime,' meaning that old media advertising income has been decimated by the Internet. It's true. But the challenge is to take an analog dollar, turn it into a digital dime, and then into a digital quarter, then again into a digital dollar, and finally into two digital dollars. That is what needs to happen and I believe it is possible."

Borthwick speaks with the same enthusiasm he had when he first saw the World Wide Web in 1993. "I was studying for my MBA at the University of Pennsylvania's Wharton School," he remembers. "A friend who worked at the Artificial Intelligence Lab at MIT in Boston called to tell me that his computer was connected to the web and he invited me to go and see it. I jumped into my car and drove for six hours from Philadelphia to Boston. It was a crazy thing to do but well worth it." Born in Britain, Borthwick came to the U.S. in 1983 to study. First he attended Wesleyan University and then Wharton. "At that time, my country was paralyzed by zero innovation and huge unemployment. Margaret Thatcher was trying to change the situation, but I was no fan of hers and I was looking for new, more exciting opportunities." Borthwick never looked back, and in 1994 he founded his first startup, Web Partners Studio, that managed three sites including Total New York, one of the first local online guides. Three years later it was bought by AOL, by then the most popular online service, and Borthwick continued to work for them becoming chief technology officer after the merger of AOL and Time Warner. "I left in 2006 and took a six-month vacation on Lake Como in Italy with my wife and our three children. It was a period of reflection," says Borthwick. "I was thinking about my next move. I wondered if I could do it in

Italy or London but unfortunately there wasn't an advanced-enough technological community in either place. And a project like Betaworks can only be built in osmosis with a high-tech community just like the current one in New York."

Among the 30 or so startups launched by Betaworks, the two most successful so far are Bit.ly and Chartbeat. "Bit.ly has over 200 million monthly users and offers interesting data on the social net," explains Borthwick. "Chartbeat is an analytical instrument used by all the principal media in the world to monitor in real time how their sites are used and how well they manage to socially involve their users." And among the latest of Borthwick's impossible undertakings is the attempt to reinvent one of the first "brands" of the social web, Digg.

Digg was created in 2004 as a way for consumers to combine news and other information on the net based on their own tastes, and to share their picks with friends. But then Digg had run its course and closed in the summer of 2012. "We bought the site, which still has an excellent brand name. Digg was a pioneer of Web 2.0, and we want to make it the answer to a real problem: the lack of a place where you can see what is discussed on the net right now, in any field. Google News is 'old'; it's our turn now."

If Betaworks calls itself a "fashion studio," there is another startup that has ties with the fashion world: Medialets. Its headquarters are located in a "sexy building," says Medialets' founder, Eric Litman, with a note of pride in his voice. And he's not wrong. When you enter 450 West 15th Street, you find an enormous art gallery on the ground floor, part of MILK Studios, a group of photographic studios that take up the whole building. And if you come during Fashion Week in February or September, you might get crushed by the trendy crowd going to the hottest shows and parties in town.

The offices of Medialets are on the floor above the gallery.

Medialets is a platform for the creation of advertising that can be viewed on mobile devices, from iPhones to iPads to Android-based products. Founded in 2008 Medialets has now 70 employees. Its technology helped create ad campaigns for the Toyota Prius, and for the launch of the third season of HBO's TV series *True Blood*.

"Everyone is trying to make mobile advertising interesting. The problem is doing it well," says Litman, a 39-year-old Los Angeles native "addicted" to technology since he was a kid in awe of his stepmom who worked for an aerospace company. While he was still in college, Litman was lucky enough to go work for NeXT, the computer company formed by Steve Jobs in 1985 after he was fired from Apple. "What I learned from him is that you can't build a successful company if you are easily pleased: you have to aim at being the best," he adds. After several jobs in the 1990s working for the first Internet companies in the service and marketing fields, and a job as manager of WashingtonVC, an incubator and investment fund located in D.C., Eric came to New York. "I fell in love with the city and with New Yorkers," says Litman. "People work here like nowhere else. When Medialets began, I stayed in the office 24 hours a day and slept on the floor, but I was happy."[4]

For three weeks straight in April 1951, without sleeping and without eating, only kept awake by gallons of coffee and other not so legal stimulants, Jack Kerouac wrote the first draft of *On the Road* in one go. At least so says the legend of the Chelsea Hotel where the beat generation poet lived at the time, and where for decades, artists, musicians, actors and writers have enlivened the bohemian life of its namesake neighborhood.

Kerouac's typewriter is one of the images in the mile-long mural of Chelsea's history that wrapped the scaffolding on Google's New York headquarters in the spring and summer of 2012. An artistic way—thanks to the work of Dark Igloo design studio of Williamsburg (Brooklyn)—to make something as monotonous as periodically checking the façade of high-rises (as required by NYC municipal law), into something entertaining.[5]

According to Google's website, which boasts of the records and the beauty of its building, it takes nine minutes to walk around the building and see the whole mural. You start out at 111 8th Avenue, and walk north to 16th street, then west to 9th Avenue where the main entrance is located at number 76. Then you continue south to West 15th and you're back at your starting point. It is an Art Deco building that dates from the 1930s, occupies a square block, and has 17 floors, many as big as two football fields, for a total of 2.9 million square feet. Until the 1970s, it housed the Port Authority of New York and New Jersey. Google moved into the building in 2006, at first only occupying a few offices and then, as it continued to grow, it decided to buy the whole building in December 2010 for $1.9 billion.

Today, just over 3,000 Googlers work in the building in a creative environment where the hip lifestyle of the twenty-to-thirty-somethings who come to work in shorts and flip-flops meet the rigor of the algorithms that are at the heart of the Internet giant's business. Nothing is boring; everything is in motion, each detail scrutinized to stimulate the minds and the imaginations of the people who work there. Parked at the entrance of each floor, a fleet of scooters is available to move employees from one part of the immense office space to another. What is more, each floor reveals its own interior design theme linked to a particular idea. The fifth floor theme for example, is "old New York." The large dining room is designed as if it were on the roof of a building, including the typical wooden water tower that is part of the New York skyline, and even fake pigeons. A puzzle that goes from one end of the floor to the other has been incorporated into the parquet and only the engineers are up to solving it.

Two of the conference rooms have a theme. They are furnished as if they were typical New York studio apartments— one where a 20-year-old male lives complete with sofa, his bicycle leaning against the wall, and laundry strewn about; the other is meant to be that of a woman, with a kitchenette that is neat and tidy—probably because she always eats out. There is also a library with a virtual bookshelf with eBooks that can be purchased using a smartphone. And there is a wall of physical books too, but it hides a secret passage to a relaxation room.

There are normal office desks, but they are not the only places where Googlers work. In fact, hardly anyone has his or her own desk. The idea behind the design of the space is to encourage informal meetings and exchange of ideas. That is Google's philosophy and it is the same in Silicon Valley, as well as in all Google offices worldwide. But here in New York, the second most important Google center, it has a special meaning. "It's true, there are differences in being a Googler in New York," states the website. "This is the capital of finance and fashion, of publishing and theater. And it makes a subtle difference in how we communicate and how fast we work. It's difficult to put into words but you always know you are in New York." And for many young people the idea of going to a bar on foot or walking to a gallery to enjoy an exhibit at the end of a tiring work day is much more attractive than commuting in the traffic of the San Francisco Bay area to get to and from the Googleplex, the Silicon Valley headquarters.

Google's first outpost in the Big Apple was opened by Tim Armstrong, the current CEO of AOL, in 2000. He was selling advertising, working out of a Starbucks on the corner of 86th and Columbus Avenue. The first engineers were hired in 2003, and the first offices were in Times Square. Today half of the staff spends its time on advertising, working closely with ad agencies and the media. The other half works on creating new products and projects, from system software to applications. And the organization keeps growing: since 2008, some Googlers have had to work in the adjacent Chelsea Market (in a space of almost fifty five thousand square feet) waiting for space at 111 Eigth Avenue to free up when the current tenants' leases expire.

New recruits are typically from East Coast universities. They are chosen through an extremely competitive process. In the summer of 2012 for example, Google held in New York the final phase of an annual contest for young programmers. Thirty-six thousand developers, aspiring Googlers, entered the contest. Eventually, the 25 surviving programmers had to challenge one another solving a variety of algorithmic problems for several hours. One of the tasks was to find the optimal way to destroy an army of zombies marching on their computer screens. The prize was ten thousand dollars, and the chance to interview with Google. A young Polish programmer, Jakub Pachocki, won. But nothing says he'll become a Googler, given New York's hunger for excellent coders and the stiff competition from other high-tech companies to get them. [6]

Another Chelsea personality with a grandiose plan is David S. Rose, who founded New York Angels in 2004 as well as AngelSoft, renamed Gust in 2011, a startup that currently takes up most of his energy, which seems otherwise inexhaustible. "You think I'm hyper now? Wrong. This is the calm me!" exclaims Rose after a torrent of words lasting an hour. He sits before a gigantic screen that shows how Gust works. Gust headquarters are on 29th Street, three blocks from the High Line. There are also offices in Vancouver, B.C., and Paris. "There are 100 million real entrepreneurs in the world, another 100 million potential investors and the Internet in the middle. The chance to connect the two groups, creating value, is enormous," explains Rose. "In seven and a half years I managed to gain the trust of all the major associations of angel investors in the U.S. and other countries, from Canada to Australia, from France to Turkey. They all use Gust software to manage their activities, and starting last year the platform has been open to entrepreneurs who are seeking financing. The interested parties can exchange information, work together, and develop their relationship online in a safe environment. It is the Big Bang of a new era for the worldwide ecosystem of entrepreneurship. We have already signed up 165,000 startups, 42,000 individual accredited investors, 300 venture capital funds, about 50 incubators as well as 800 groups of angel investors," says Rose, who dreams of adding lawyers and accountants, investment bankers, and large investors to his super-sized database. In other words, all the stakeholders in the startup world.[7]

Sex and power, fashion and high-tech, but also wealth and patronage are personified by the most famous power couple at the center of the rebirth of the Meatpacking District and Chelsea—Diane von Furstenberg and Barry Diller, the *fashionista* who designed the "wrap dress" and the ex Hollywood mogul who reinvented himself as an Internet tycoon with his InterActive Corp. (IAC) holding company founded in 1996. Diane (65 years old) and Barry (70 years old), who married in 2001, have so far donated $35 million to build and maintain the High Line, the elevated park built on the abandoned tracks of a now-defunct freight line that ran from Gansevoort to 30th Street along 10th Avenue. The last part of the donation, some $20 million, was announced in October 2011 to complete work on the project. At the time it was the largest donation ever given to a New York park, surpassed only in 2012 by a $100 million donation to Central Park from John Paulson.

The High Line, inaugurated in June 2009, has become a destination both for tourists and for New Yorkers looking for a breath of fresh air, green landscapes, post-industrial scenery, futuristic architecture, and art installations. Looking east you can see the Diane von Furstenberg's (DvF) offices with the ground floor boutique on Washington Street. To the west, almost on the Hudson River, you see IAC's headquarters, the unmistakable Frank Gehry building that opened in 2007, its irregular shape illuminated at night. About 50 Internet companies are located there, including Ask.com, an online question and answer engine, Match.com, a dating service, Urbanspoon, a restaurant guide, and Newsweek with The Daily Beast. Altogether, they have over 300 million unique visitors per month in 30 countries. Some of the companies, such as Ask.com, created in 1996, are dot-com bubble survivors. Others are new generation Internet companies such as OkCupid, another Internet dating site that was launched in 2004.

A pioneer who wants to push the boundaries of the New York digital boom even farther west is John Katzman, 52 years old. He is well known in the groves of American academe as the founder of *The Princeton Review*, first published in 1981 and still the "bible" for many families with college-bound kids who need to prepare for the SATs and submit their applications. With an athletic, hockey player's build, Katzman found a place for his startup 2tor (now known as 2U)—as well as his other startup, Noodle Education, that aims to become the ultimate search engine for everything education related—at Chelsea Piers, the sports complex on the Hudson River south of 23rd Street. "I used to come here to watch hockey, so I got to know the managers and they rented the office space to me," recalls Katzman. "It's a fantastic place with a great view over the river. I would like to bring at least five hundred people from the technological community here."

Katzman was born and raised in New York and is attached to the West Side, where he has lived most of his life. He created The Princeton Review when he was 21, just after graduating from Princeton. The business grew and became a public company in 2001, against Katzman's better judgment: "it was a bad idea with too many costs and management problems," he recalls. "I left the company in 2007 and began 2tor with three million dollars of my own money." 2tor is a new model of postgraduate online university programs. The first was launched in June 2009 in collaboration with the University of Southern California; other university partners today include Georgetown University and the University of North Carolina, both offering MBAs online as well as other degrees. "Other schools and other sites have tried offering online degrees and failed or turned out to be low quality because the promoters themselves didn't believe in them, they weren't convinced that online courses could be as good as those on campus," maintains Katzman. "But I'm certain that the future of higher education is online; it is the only way to reduce the exploding cost of a college education that is now totally out of control." Many venture capitalists believe the same thing—a fact attested to by the almost $100 million invested in his project. Perhaps one day Katzman will succeed in producing such a brilliant online course to convince Miller, and other college dropouts like him, to get their degrees rather than following the example of Steve Jobs who gave up going to "useless" college.[8]

6

The Boheme of the Third Millennium

East Village, Soho and Lower Manhattan

The famous musical *Rent* celebrated the Bohemian life of New York in the 1980s, with the penniless artists who could not pay the rent on their lofts. They spent their nights at the Life Café in Alphabet City, where the bartender would try and push them out because they couldn't even buy a cup of coffee. One of them was Mark, who dreamed of producing his own documentary.

Today Mark wouldn't have any problem working on it all day long on his laptop at Tom & Jerry's, using their free wi-fi and swapping ideas with the other self-starters who are using the place as their office—and who knows, he might even find someone to finance his project. Tom & Jerry, at 288 Elizabeth Street, just a few blocks away from where the now-closed Life Café was located, is in fact "the best bar to rub elbows with a venture capitalist in New York."[1] It's also a favorite hangout of Dennis Crowley's and his team at Foursquare, with offices just a ten-minute walk away, as well as many other entrepreneurs in the digital business.

The times described by *Rent*—when areas of downtown Manhattan such as Alphabet City were dangerous places to visit at night and a junkie could easily mug you—are now history.

But the desire to create something out of nothing still hangs in the air around the founders of young companies that have a presence here as well. It is here that Scott Heiferman founded Meetup in 2002. And not by chance Meetup's motto is "DIO: Do It Ourselves." And doing it themselves is the road chosen by many new entrepreneurs who "bootstrap" their companies, keeping expenses to a minimum and avoiding to turn to outside investors as long as possible.

Today, it is easier to manage this thanks to the availability of co-working spaces as WeWork Labs on Varick Street near Soho. Zemanta has offices there together with thirty other startups. There are also programs such as the TechStars accelerator in Cooper Square. It is just steps away from the Interactive Telecommunications Program (ITP) at the Tisch School of the Arts at New York University, a breeding ground of ideas for the New York high-tech community since the 1990s. And in order to find alternative ways to solve their financing problems, the startups can turn to the support of those who are opening new avenues—such as Kickstarter, located on the lower East Side, whose mission is to "help people finance creative projects," as stated on its website. SecondMarket, the market for private company stock, is just steps away from Wall Street.

Dennis Crowley, 36 years old, with an open smile and 1960s Beatles-style hair, founded his first company, Dodgeball, with a fellow student, Alex Rainert, in 2003 while studying for a Master's at ITP). "There were a lot of people at ITP who had worked at dot-com companies and lost their jobs when the bubble burst," Crowley recalls. "I was writing software programs for my schoolmates." Dodgeball was one of the first social networking services for mobile devices based on "location." In practice, it was the precursor of Foursquare. Google bought it in 2005 and Crowley and Rainert continued to work there until 2007 when both of them left, frustrated by the limited involvement of their new boss in developing the startup.

"Google might have preferred us to move out to Silicon Valley but we wanted to stay in New York where our families and friends are," says Crowley. "New York is a fantastic city when you figure out how to make it work for you—how to go skiing in the winter and to the beach in the summer and how to choose between millions of places like bars and restaurants. Foursquare evolved from this practical problem; it is an instrument that makes it easier and more interesting to live in a city, and it's a better product because it was developed here and had to solve the special problems of such a heavily populated area." Among the many problems is that of the GPS (Global Positioning System) that works badly because of the many high-rises in Manhattan. GPS is an obvious must for a social network based on geographic localization such as Foursquare. "If you can create software that gets past these obstacles then you'll do well anywhere," says Crowley.

While working for another startup after leaving Google, Crowley met his future partner, Naveen Selvadurai. They shared office space in Manhattan; both lived in the East Village, and had the same problem of where to meet friends for a drink. So at the beginning of 2009 Crowley dusted off the old Dodgeball project, shut down by Google in the meantime, and working with Selvadurai they created Foursquare in just three months. It's a smartphone application that lets you "check in" everywhere you go so your friends can know where you are. Moreover it gives you suggestions of where to go based on your tastes and those of your friends. And, more recently, it gives merchants the chance to offer special promotions and discounts to attract potential customers who have been located in their neighborhood. So it is now beginning to make money.

Created at the kitchen table in Crowley's loft, Foursquare now occupies two floors of a building at the corner of Broadway and Prince Street, where about one hundred people work with another thirty working in San Francisco. There are large open spaces where Crowley, the CEO, sits in the middle with the rest of the team, changing places every so often so as to be directly in touch with his employees, listening to their ideas and their problems. There is a giant screen in the large dining room for teleconferences but also for watching events like the Olympics on TV while chatting with co-workers or working on your laptop and, of course, it is where the company holds conferences or events.

"We are just at the beginning of the journey to becoming a large social networking company. We are growing at the rate of one million new users a month," says Crowley while he refutes any idea of an IPO or a sale to a third party. Foursquare's "friends" now number more than 20 million and 60% of them are outside the U.S. So far angel investors and venture capitalists have financed them to the tune of $71 million, at a valuation of $600 million.

"Founding Dodgeball was really hard because at that time I had to do everything myself," remembers Crowley. "Now the New York technological community is much stronger, thanks to Google drawing so many engineers here to New York. A third of the people who work with me are ex-Googlers. And there's a great feeling of cooperation and collaboration."

If competition among entrepreneurs is the soul of innovation, here in New York you can taste a version combined with a sincere spirit of comradeship. "Many people who, like me, have experience in other startups, dedicate part of their time to helping the kids who are just starting out," says Crowley. "A couple of mornings a week I grab a cup of coffee with someone who has asked me for advice, I speak at a conference or mentor for programs like TechStars. I explain how important it is to manage your mood in the highs and lows on the road to creating a startup—something that is not as glamorous as what people saw in the movie *The Social Network*. You are often afraid and think 'Oh my god, the other startups are killing us.' But you've got to remember that the others are thinking the same thing about you and so you have to believe in what you're doing."[2]

It's not easy to get into TechStars. "We are more selective than an Ivy League school," advises their website. More than 1,500 aspiring entrepreneurs applied for the spring 2012 program in New York but only thirteen were accepted to the Cooper Square campus co-founded by David Tisch. Those who make it receive $118,000 startup capital and three months of full immersion in the New York technological community where they learn the ABCs of how to start a company. At the end of the program they have a chance to present their company to potential investors. The 11 "graduates" of the first course, organized in the winter of 2010-2011, raised over $22 million dollars in financing. The 12 graduates of the summer 2011 course raised almost $14 million and so far the 13 in the spring 2012 class have raised five million. Only two have failed so far.

"But it's OK to fail, it's part of the lessons you have to learn and if you have talent and have worked seriously on your project, you can always build a high-tech career for yourself in New York. You can count on someone giving you a job," says Tisch, who is 30 years old and a scion of one of the richest families in the U.S. The family controls, among other things, the Loews Hotel chain and donated the building where the Tisch School of the Arts is located, just steps away from TechStars.

What's the proof that you can always pick yourself up in the event of failure? Starting a company and failing is one of the five criteria the founder of TechStars, David Cohen, uses to choose his program managers. The others are: starting a successful company; investing in a startup; raising venture capital; being from the city where the program is taking place. "'I comply with three of these criteria and I might not qualify as I haven't started a successful business or raised capital but I would be very interested,' I told Cohen the first time we met at an angel bootcamp in Boston in May 2010," relays Tisch. "I had approached him somewhat clumsily, asking him point blank, 'How come you're not in New York?' TechStars was created in 2006 in Boulder, Colorado and I had carefully studied the experience, as I have always been fascinated by computers and by the idea of having my own Internet company or being an investor in the field—but I didn't know how to go about it."

Tisch, who started using computers in the early '90s ("I got my first Mac in fourth grade and I learned the AppleScript language to access AOL for free"), got the idea of creating a site that specialized in the real estate market in 2007 but then gave it up, and went to work for New York-based BPO (Business Process Outsourcing) company KGB, where he remained until 2009. "But in the meantime I became an angel investor with one of my companies, Box Group, and began thinking about founding something similar to TechStars or Y Combinator in California. So I met up with Cohen, whom I trusted, and he invited me to Boulder for a week so we could get to know each other better. I flew out there and after a month, in August 2010, I became the managing director of new programs in New York. The difficult part is choosing from among the many applications. It's an intense process that lasts six months and it's 24/7 week after week after week."

There's no entrance exam but the waiting list is long if you want to find a desk or office space at WeWork Labs, a co-working space founded in April 2011 by three partners. Zemanta is one of the thirty-some startups that work there, taking advantage of the common areas, including those for relaxing. There's a room with a ping-pong table, a pinball machine and a foosball table. "When people are playing they make a lot of noise," confides Boštjan Špetič, founder and CEO of Zemanta. "Sometimes I think about launching my own co-working space for European startups interested in establishing themselves in New York. Something calmer, with good coffee and with assistance for those who come here and have to quickly learn how things are done in the States." Špetič is 29 years old and a native of Ljubljana, Slovenia (former Yugoslavia). That is where he first began working on the Internet in 2001, in the first cyber café at the university where he was studying philosophy. In 2007, he and his friend Andraž Tori won a competition organized by Seedcamp in London. That is where Zemanta was created. It is software that helps bloggers and anyone else who produces content on the web to make their pages look better with images and intelligent links. "We found our first investors, Eden Ventures, in London and we even got some attention from the U.S.," says Špetič. "Fred Wilson of Union Square Ventures called us in summer 2008 and convinced us to move to New York, becoming our second big investor." Špetič immediately flew to the States, and in January 2009 began hiring people for marketing and sales while the engineers and developers stayed in Ljubljana.

"Times were hard, after the Lehman debacle, and every week another publisher was having problems. This was bad news for us as we were looking for media clients," remembers Špetič. "But I was immediately fascinated by the business culture I found here. Everybody listens to you, even important people agree to meet you, and after hearing you out, they quickly tell you what they think of your proposal. It's much more rational than in Europe where you waste a lot of time in interminable meetings without getting any results."

But one of the biggest problems for the founder of a non-American startup is getting a visa to work in the U.S. Huge obstacles are thrown in your path and without a good lawyer you run the risk of what happened to Špetič. Renewal of his visa was denied in the fall of 2010 even though Zemanta was starting to show a profit with a new business model based on "sponsored recommendations" from businesses. So for three months he had to work out of Ljubljana, until his new lawyer found the key to getting him back to New York where he now has 10 employees, while another 20 work in Slovenia. "We have several Russians, who have run away from their country, working for us in Ljubljana and we also have a few Americans who want to spend some time in Europe," says Špetič. "It's not easy managing the two teams from so far away, with the six hour time difference and the different cultures, European versus American, as well as marketing versus engineering. We had a lot of communication problems in 2010, and now I try to stay on top of things and so I hold a videoconference meeting every Monday, I go to Ljubljana once every two months and I send all the New Yorkers there for one week a year to foster team spirit."[3]

Having your technical staff in your native country and your business staff in the U.S. has been a model successfully used by Israeli startups for a number of years. Mobli does this as well: it is one of the most frequently cited social networks in the gossip columns on the Manhattan party circuit. It is well-known because its investors include the actors Leonardo DiCaprio and Toby Maguire, the tennis star Serena Williams and other celebs. It is located in the southernmost part of the city, not far from DiCaprio's Battery Park City apartment. He was the first to step up, with an investment of four million dollars so far.

Its founder, Moshe Hogeg, thinks big and wants to make Mobli the Google "of everything that is worth seeing in the world"; in other words, a visual search engine that can display images and video, in real time—see the world through other people's eyes. Hogeg, born 31 years ago in Beersheba in the south of Israel, claims enthusiastically "it could change the world." As a boy he liked to infiltrate chat rooms to sabotage the computers of people who called themselves Hitler or other Nazi names. He enlisted in the army after finishing high school and at the age of 24 he became an officer in charge of 125 soldiers and an annual budget of millions of dollars. "Technology is the real strength of our armed forces," says Hogeg. "I created a sort of military eBay for the army to sell decommissioned material that was still usable. They saved sixty million dollars a year and they gave me a reward of …five thousand dollars! OK, I said to myself, time to go off on my own." After leaving the army in 2009 he had an inspiration. "While I was at a concert, I received a text message from my sister. It said, 'Wish I was there.' All around me there were thousands of people taking photos with their smartphones and I thought there must be as many eyes that could 'see' the show on behalf of my sister or anyone else. I just had to connect them." And that is what Mobli does. It's an app for sharing photos and videos, even with people not connected through Facebook or Twitter, organized by subject and where the photos originated. "We are now working with face and place recognition technologies to develop a visual search engine, different from Google Images," explains Hogeg. "If you use Google to find a photo of DiCaprio, you probably get one of him on the Titanic; with Mobli you get one taken by someone who just saw him walk out of his house or walking down the street."

Hogeg met DiCaprio in 2011, the year he moved to New York hunting for investors. "I had begun in Israel, penniless, working out of my home, convincing four technical guys to work for me in exchange for a piece of the startup," relates Hogeg. "I had also found an Israeli angel investor but Israel has little experience in the Internet sector for consumers. I knew the CEO of a large insurance company in New York and he became my partner and I also hoped to convince some big names to help in launching Mobli. I was lucky. By chance DiCaprio saw a friend of his doing a test using our app and he liked it immensely, so much so that he asked to meet me. What a dream! We met at his New York apartment and he explained that investing in Mobli was part of his 'business model' and he thought that the platform could be useful for his brand." Thanks to that support, Mobli reached three million users in less than a year. It has twenty employees in Israel, fifteen in Manhattan and has no intention of moving out to Silicon Valley to be closer to Hollywood. "It's easier here for the time zones," explains Hogeg, "and we feel the environment is special, that it is pushing us to become a great Internet company."[4]

Practically across the street from Mobli and just a few yards away from the "Bull" of Wall Street you find SecondMarket, the alternative trading system where Facebook shares went sky-high (more than $40 per share) before its IPO in May 2012. SecondMarket is where private company shares, not yet offered on public stock exchanges, can be traded. Two of the best known New York companies traded on SecondMarket are Foursquare and Gilt Groupe. Some analysts have accused SecondMarket of being the market of the new Internet bubble and of having been instrumental in determining—or "inflating," depending on one's point of view—the pricing of Facebook's IPO. Hence SecondMarket is held partially responsible for Facebook's share price collapse from its offering price of $38 per share to a low of $17.55 just four months later.

But SecondMarket founder Barry Silbert, 35, is unperturbed: he notes that LinkedIn had traded on his market and subsequently had a successful public performance (+130% one year after the IPO). On the other hand, Zynga and Pandora never traded on SecondMarket, they went public and then cratered on Nasdaq. So there is no correlation, according to him, between SecondMarket's role and the post-IPO performance of the companies that trade on it. Silbert explains what is his true mission: to respond to the need of technology startups to make their stock "liquid" without having to do a public offering—a process that has become very expensive and much more bureaucratic after the introduction of the Sarbanes-Oxley Act of 2002. The time lag from company inception to a public offering has gone from four and a half years on average in the '90s to 10 years currently. But in the meantime many employees who are rewarded with stock options, as it is typical in the high-tech sector, want to be able to cash out. In fact, a former employee of Facebook, who needed to sell his shares, drove Silbert to start this market in 2009.

A native of Maryland, fatherless at age 11, financial broker at 17 to help his mother make ends meet, Silber graduated from Emory University in Atlanta with a degree in business. While working at the Los Angeles investment bank Houlihan Lokey he specialized in illiquid securities. He also handled the sale of Enron's assets after the crash of 2001. From there he got the idea to create an "eBay for shares of private companies." In fact SecondMarket, founded in 2004, operates as an auction: the "listed" company gives the ok on each sale of its stock and supplies its audited financial statements to investors, who can only be institutions (such as pension funds and hedge funds) or accredited individual investors with financial assets of at least one million dollars. No small investor can lose his shirt on this exchange.

There are 130 employees working at SecondMarket, among them brokers, engineers, lawyers and administrative personnel. The environment is half way between Wall Street and Silicon Valley: from the trading floor filled with financial terminals, you can walk into a lounge where Silbert and colleagues eat and play ping-pong or air-hockey. There were 150 employees until March 2012, when Silbert decided to cut the work force by 10% to compensate for the drop in business after Facebook's IPO. But this was not entirely bad news for SecondMarket. "We've never had so many companies engaging with us. They're looking at what's happening in the public market with the way stocks from recent IPOs are getting pummeled, and the way that the management teams are getting destroyed in the press, and want nothing to do with it," said Silbert in August 2012.[5][6]

A completely atypical exchange, where you can finance the most disparate dreams, is Kickstarter. Here Mark, the protagonist of *Rent*, could have gathered enough money to produce his documentary. In fact, the idea of founding it came to Perry Chen while he was trying to organize a concert. Chen, a fan of electronic music, in 2002 lived in New Orleans. He realized he needed a few thousand dollars, which he did not have, and he did not want to borrow money with the risk of not having enough of an audience to pay back his expenses. The solution would be—he thought then—to know beforehand how many people were willing to pay for tickets. Seven years of "wandering" went by from idea to startup, during which Chen was between New Orleans—the city of music and artistic entertainment—and New York—the city of "ambition," as 36-years-old Chen likes to say. He found his partners by accident, while he was working as a waiter at a restaurant in Brooklyn: Yancey Strickler, a music journalist, and Charles Adler, a designer. The first investor was the actor David Cross, a cousin of a friend of Chen's, who was followed by other friends in the arts.

Not surprisingly, music or movie production projects are the most popular on Kickstarter. Since its launch in 2009, the company has been used to promote nearly 70,000 initiatives in the most diverse fields, including technology: nearly half have been successful, collecting more than $260 million from about three million small "benefactors." The mechanism is simple: anyone who has a project that fits Kickstarter's guidelines (excluding investments, philanthropy and now certain product categories) can submit it on the site explaining how much money it needs to raise and what it expects to give in return for the patron's support (an autographed and personalized copy of the book being written, for instance); the idea has 60 days to collect enough commitments and, if it reaches its goal, the project is funded and the supporters' credit cards are charged: transparent and without risk for everyone involved. The average project costs $10,000, and the most common donation is around $10. But some initiatives have already collected over one million dollars. The most famous is the creature of a 25-year-old designer from Palo Alto, Eric Migicovsky: a customizable watch that connects wirelessly to your smartphone. Asking $100,000 to start manufacturing it has collected, instead, between April and May 2012, $10 million from nearly 70,000 enthusiastic potential customers willing to pay $115 or more for each "Pebble."[7]

Chen describes Kickstarter as something between altruism and capitalism. People commit to contributing money not hoping for a gain, but because they like the idea or the people behind it; as compensation you expect an enjoyable experience or the satisfaction of having participated in the birth of a cool product. Kickstarter, on the other hand, is not a nonprofit organization: it is in the black, collecting 5% of the funds raised. And it counts among its backers the cream of American angel investors and venture capital funds, from Scott Heiferman of Meetup, to Jack Dorsey of Twitter, to Fred Wilson and Union Square Ventures, for a total of $10 million.

At the moment design and technology projects offered on Kickstarter account for only 5% of the total, but that number is growing quickly. It is a way for inventors to test their prototypes while minimizing risk and costs, turning directly to consumers and skipping traditional middlemen such as banks, who are more and more reluctant to provide funding. It is a model that appeals to Brooklyn's flourishing "maker movement." That might be why Chen decided to move his offices from the Lower East Side to Greenpoint, Brooklyn where he bought an old factory building in August 2012. It is an abandoned structure badly in need of renovation. The factory made pencils, an object that for generations was a symbol of how children became students and then better people. It will be the source of a new, intangible but even more powerful tool of emancipation—the network of ideas, from dream to creation.[8]

7
The Do-It-Yourself Revolution
Brooklyn

Their preferred form of transportation is the bicycle. They are "locavores," meaning they eat and drink locally grown products. They buy artisan-made clothes and furnish their lofts with artisanal wares. And many of them have rediscovered the pleasure of making things by hand, but without giving up the most sophisticated instruments of the digital era. In fact, they use the power of the Internet to pursue their dreams.

They are the creative young people who live and work in Brooklyn at the over 500 startups in the Tech Triangle, defined by its vertices in Dumbo, the MetroTech Center downtown and the Brooklyn Navy Yard, the old naval yard converted into an industrial park. It is a universe of companies worth three billion dollars to the local economy and provides 33,000 jobs between direct jobs (almost 10,000) and indirect ones, according to estimates from the first study of the area, published by Urbanomics in April 2012.[1]

Etsy and MakerBot are the startups that best express the unique spirit of "Made in Brooklyn" high-tech. The former is an online market of products that are strictly hand-made and the latter is a producer of 3D printers "for the masses." These are two successful businesses where profits increase along with a political message. Etsy CEO Chad Dickerson talks of a quiet revolution to bring human beings back to the center of the economy, while MakerBot CEO Bre Pettis is an evangelist of "the maker movement," that is people who create, invent, repair, transform or improve things as a way of stimulating innovation and entrepreneurship. The common thread is the criticism of the model of capitalism that took us into the Great Recession and the search for a way out, using the ingenuity of the individual. And having fun doing it!

To be clear, the Brooklyn creative minds are not penitent monks. They live here not only because it is less expensive, but also because of its more relaxed, romantic atmosphere in contrast to the frenetic rhythms of Manhattan.

Up until the end of the 1990s, Dumbo was strictly the reign of a group of avant-garde artists who had taken over the abandoned factories and warehouses and were happy that their value was not appreciating as had happened to Soho in Manhattan, where rents and the cost of living had gone way up. These artists, the pioneers of the 70s and 80s, had coined the acronym Dumbo, for "Down Under the Manhattan Bridge Overpass," with the obvious pejorative connotation of someone who is "thick," in the hope that such a name would keep speculators away from the area.

It was the city of New York itself that caused the transformation when, in 1998, it decided to change the zoning of Dumbo from industrial to mixed-use, thus allowing the buildings to be converted for residential and commercial use, besides light industrial use. But, fortunately for the area, David Walentas was the property developer: through his Two Trees Management company, he had bought almost all of the buildings at rock-bottom prices in 1981. When Walentas was finally able to renovate them he did it intelligently, maintaining their post-industrial appeal and anticipating that Dumbo would officially be designated a historic landmark, which happened in 2007.[2]

One of the first companies to settle here in 1999 was Huge, a digital advertising and marketing agency that now employs four hundred people in its offices at 20 Jay Street. It was taken over by the Interpublic Group of Companies in 2008. Since '99 over sixty agencies that specialize in digital advertising and marketing such as Big Spaceship, Red Antler, and Carrot Creative have either been created or moved into the area. Movie director Spike Lee founded one of the most recent, Spike DDB, in 2009.[3]

These companies are attracted to the area by the price of office space, much lower than in Manhattan, although it is really nearby, just one stop away on the subway. In addition, there are tax incentives to settle in Brooklyn. "But more than anything else I think the magnet is the creative DNA found in Dumbo. A number of designers and software developers as well as artists, musicians, writers and other creative types in all fields have chosen to live here," explains Micah Kotch, who was born in Brooklyn 35 years ago. Today he is the director of operations at NYU-Poly DUMBO Incubator, taking up a whole floor in the same building as Huge, just steps away from the East River. The building was put up at the beginning of the 20th century and was once part of the Arbuckle Coffee roasting factory. Now it is home to Howaboutwe.com[4], an online dating service, among others. It also houses the DUMBO Improvement District[5], a reference point for those who live and work in the area.

"Dumbo's transformation is incredible," says Kotch. "When I was a kid this wasn't the kind of place you wanted to hang out in, apart from my high school days when we'd come here to drink beer under the bridge. Now it's an area with its own kind of energy, different from Manhattan. But that doesn't mean that people here don't work as hard. The intensity, the thoroughness, the time and ambition dedicated to working are the same here as on the other side of the river."

That energy has its own rituals for letting off steam. The monthly meetings organized by Digital DUMBO are the best attended. It's the Dumbo way of networking with a bottle of local micro-brewery beer in hand and high-volume music playing in the large room at Dumbo Loft on Water Street. From 300 to 600 people are there for each event; people who already have a job or those who are looking for work in a startup, students, friends, or the simply curious. But you can also find talent scout investors, on the lookout for new entrepreneurs.[6]

"At the July 2010 meeting Sam Lessin presented his startup, Drop.io, a file-sharing service for online collaboration created here in Dumbo. It might just be a coincidence, but two months later it was bought by Facebook," proudly recalls the soul of Digital DUMBO, Andrew Zarick. Presently, he is contemplating the idea of exporting the model of his meetings to other creative centers in the world, such as Berlin or London.

Among the sponsors of these meetings is the NYU-Poly DUMBO Incubator, that opened its doors in January 2012 and six months later had already hosted twelve startups. "We specialize in the digital media and digital gaming sectors that are at the heart of this technological community," explains Kotch. The city of New York gave him the resources to start; the office space is Two Trees Management's, and administration is carried out by NYU-Poly. NYU-Poly was formed in 2008 through a merger of the Polytechnic Institute of New York, the second-oldest private engineering school in the U.S., founded in Brooklyn in 1854, and the New York University School of Engineering. "As soon as we opened, we received two hundred applications, and we chose the first projects in accordance with university research interests," says Kotch. "We supply all the services needed to open a business, from legal consultation to introductions to potential investors, and also talent, that is university professors to act as mentors and students for internships."

The original mix of idealism and business at Dumbo is well-expressed by one of the startups at the incubator: Docracy—from documents and democracy—is a free service, just like a Wikipedia of the most common legal documents used by individuals, e.g. wills, and by professionals or entrepreneurs, e.g. standard contracts. "The first version of Docracy was created one night during a TechCrunch hackathon, a contest for programmers that we won," say Matt Hall and John Watkinson. "The idea came to us from our earlier adventures as small businesspeople dealing with exorbitant legal fees just for standard documents, the same for everyone." They began in an office in Manhattan but then took advantage of the incubator opportunity and moved to Dumbo because both of them live in Brooklyn. "We like it here, we can come to work on foot and it's easier to get to know people and stay in touch," explain Matt and John. And they don't care if they're not making a cent at the moment. "We hope we are useful to freelancers and others like us who are careful about how they use their budget, but also useful to lawyers who are looking for clients," add Matt and John. "Maybe one day we'll be able to add some premium content that will not be free."[7]

The company that everyone looks to for inspiration is Etsy, an online market where only handmade merchandise, made by artisans or amateurs, is on offer, both new and vintage. The range of goods varies from pearl necklaces to wood furniture, from "grandma's" jams to decorative ceramics, with prices ranging from 20 cents to $100,000. It's an unusual Internet boutique that's always open. To display your own creations you pay 20 cents per item and a 3.5% commission on everything sold. Etsy's net sales was about 50 million dollars in 2011, thanks to a volume of $525,000,000 of products sold through its website by over 800,000 active sellers in 150 countries. Almost 300 employees work in the eccentrically decorated offices at 55 Washington Street, where only things produced by its own artisans are on display. Etsy also has offices in Hudson, New York, in San Francisco and in Berlin, Germany.

Etsy was founded in 2005 by Robert Kalin, a penniless 24-year-old with a passion for do-it-yourself (DIY) and the problem of finding the right online site where he could sell his wares. He is famous among DIY enthusiasts because he still makes his own furniture and even his underwear. Kalin launched Etsy from a dilapidated loft in Dumbo together with two friends from school who were good at creating websites. It took them three months to launch the service, whose name comes from the Latin 'etsi' and means 'even if.' In the summer of 2011, Kalin left the leadership of the company to 40-year-old Chad Dickerson, who was already the chief technology officer and a believer in Etsy's philosophy. To understand it, it's a good idea to read the manifesto that was drawn up after the first conference Etsy promoted in September 2011 in Berlin. Over 500 independent business owners from 17 countries attended the conference where they discussed "human scale economies" and social entrepreneurship.

"Decades of an unyielding focus on economic growth and a corporate mentality has left us ever more disconnected with nature, our communities, and the people and processes behind the objects in our lives," writes Chad Dickerson on Etsy's blog. "We think this is unethical, unsustainable, and unfun. However, with the rise of small businesses around the world we feel hope and see real opportunities to measure success in new ways... to build local, living economies, and most importantly, to help create a more permanent future." Etsy offers itself as a model of this alternative style of "'running businesses sustainably, responsibly, and profitably, with people at the center," explains

Dickerson. "It's a type of cooperation you could call 'sharing economy' as part of a broader 'quiet revolution' and that can help businesses change the world."[8]

Utopian? Retro with a hint of environmentalist/anti-industrial bent? It is what it is, but in the meantime the angel investors and the venture capitalists believe in it. Burda, Union Square Ventures, Accel Partners, and Index Ventures have so far invested over 90 million dollars in Etsy, making it worth 600 million. To be sure, Etsy is a "B corporation" where "B" stands for benefit. This means the company uses its business power to resolve social and environmental problems, as certified by the B Lab institute. But since 2009 it has also shown a profit even though the company won't say how much.[9]

The new Center for Urban Science and Progress (CUSP) will be built at the second vertex of the Brooklyn Tech Triangle, MetroTech, where NYU-Poly is located. In addition, new enterprises inspired by the maker movement are about to open there. This is an area of downtown Brooklyn halfway between Dumbo and the Navy Yard. Just a few miles separates the most distant points of the triangle but to make it even easier for the startups to work together, the MTA (Metropolitan Transportation Authority) has okayed a new bus line to serve the technology district.

CUSP will work on solving many urban problems, such as how public transportation should be organized for a city in the new millennium. CUSP is a research institute of applied science created by a consortium of universities that includes City University of New York, Carnegie Mellon University, the University of Toronto, the University of Warwick, the Indian Institute of Technology - Bombay and of course NYU. Large technology companies such as, IBM, Cisco, Siemens and Xerox are supporters of the center. The institute will be built above the Jay Street subway station, one of the busiest in the city, where the old MTA building, abandoned and decaying for the last ten years, is located. "It's kind of poetic justice for that space to go to CUSP," comments Fred Wilson of Union Square Ventures, who is a trustee of NYU-Poly and contributor to the project. Once the renovation is completed, currently expected by 2017, the building will host 50 scientists, 400 students studying for their Master's degree and 100 doctoral candidates all under the guidance of a Brooklyn native: the theoretical physicist Steven Koonin, formerly Under Secretary of Energy for Science at the U.S. Department of Energy, and ex-provost of the California Institute of Technology.

In the fall of 2011 another experiment in the field of education and cooperation between the public and private sectors began in Crown Heights, not far from CUSP. It is also an attempt to address the demand for talented technical people from New York startups.

Called Pathways in Technology Early College High School (P-TECH), it is a kind of super-high-school that lasts for six years instead of the traditional four and grants a double diploma: the regular high school diploma and an associate degree in computer science. P-TECH is a public school run by the city of New York, City University of New York (CUNY), and IBM, which came up with the idea and donated $500,000 in software and computers while making its technical experts available as mentors to the over 100 students. The last two years are the most intense as they include company internships and professional training. Those who get their degrees after six years have a good chance at finding jobs at IBM or another company, or they can use the extra two years for college credits. This program is the first of its kind in the U.S. and IBM would like to export it to other cities, particularly in areas where unemployment is really high, such as Crown Heights itself. Initial results have been promising, with 100 students enrolled, most of them from the less well-off families in the area.

MakerBot Industries is the trendiest new tenant at the MetroTech Center. It moved here in the spring of 2012 because it had become too big (125 employees) for its original office space in Boerum Hill, the small artistic area just ten blocks south of MetroTech. Bre Pettis and two friends, all DIY enthusiasts, founded the company in January 2009. A kind of Renaissance man of the 21st century, Pettis, 40 years old, has also been a teacher, an artist and a puppeteer. Now he "makes things that make things," as he explains on his website.

A "thing that makes things" is MakerBot's product, a 3D printer/replicator that churns out objects made of materials such as the ones Lego uses and no bigger than a soccer ball. They begin with designs that customers can find for free on Thingiverse, an open-source online design community. The innovation is the price, less than $2,000 dollars per replicator, that makes it accessible to many, from hobbyists who use it for fun, to small businesses that manufacture products or prototypes, to parents who help their children with a school science project.[10]

Those who do not want to buy machinery or other tools for DIY can, for a hundred dollars a month, become members of TechShop, a chain of laboratories with all the machines needed to work on any kind of hardware, from making furniture, to repair motorcycles and create prototypes. Jim Newton opened the first Techshop in Raleigh, North Carolina in 2006. Now there are others in San Francisco, Menlo Park, San Jose, and Detroit. And another will open in the MetroTech Center in Brooklyn. "It will work as a 'gym' for startups that make material objects, an interesting new addition to our technological community," concludes Micah Kotch.[11]

The artisans at Etsy will of course take advantage of it, given that they already work with MakerBot in the same spirit of rediscovery of one's manual talent, which is at the heart of the maker movement. It is the community of "those who produce something tangible," those who create, invent, repair, transform or improve an object. The Great Recession contributed to the increasing popularity of this trend for economic reasons. As part of this, there are also those who sharpen their brains by solving problems on their own without having to pay for professional help. But, according to Pettis and his followers, there are also a growing number of people who dream of turning their passion for DIY into a profitable business, an alternative model to revitalize the old American entrepreneurial spirit.

8
Sunshine Fortress
The Bronx

Sunshine has been working the streets of Hunts Point for twenty years. She came here when she was seventeen "to taste the heroin" because she had heard it was "the best" in town. Peroxide blonde hair, a large tattoo on her ample breast saying "Thug Misses," as the rapper Khia, Sunshine says she has been clean for the last two years and dreams of "giving something positive" to the kids in this area. She is one of the prostitutes who still work this area of the South Bronx where more than 10,000 trucks pass through every night to unload fruit and vegetables, meat and fish at the largest wholesale market in New York.[1]

Hunts Point is a name that brings many different stereotypes of the Bronx to mind. HBO dedicated a documentary to its red light district, *Hookers at the Point* (2002), and the local police station, the 41st Precinct, became notorious in the film *Fort Apache, the Bronx*, where Paul Newman played a police officer who felt helpless and attacked on all sides by adversaries like a greenhorn in the Wild West. At the time of President Carter's tour of the area in 1977, the press had a field day with photos of all the burned out and abandoned buildings and the rubble-strewn streets, a symbol of urban decay that the neighborhood once epitomized.[2]

Today there are clean streets, new housing, and a much lower crime rate. But not all the problems have been solved—this, the 16th District, is still the poorest voting precinct in the U.S. Neither is the area free of gang violence. In the summer of 2012, a number of kids were killed or wounded. One of these was Lloyd Morgan, a four-year-old who was killed by a stray bullet at a playground on July 22nd.

But there is another Sunshine that stands out here: the community of small businesses and startups that works in the Bronx's first incubator. It is sponsored by the City of New York and was opened in January 2012 as a cooperative effort with two business schools, Monroe College and Baruch College. It occupies a floor in the Bank Note Building, a kind of "fortress" where the American Bank Note Company printed money in the early 1900s. In 1985, it was abandoned and left to decay, only to be taken over by illegal tenants for 20 years until finally, in December 2007, it was bought by Taconic, a real estate developer who renovated it and now rents office space to various companies and organizations.

Upon entering the enormous loft where Sunshine Bronx is located, three things strike you: the light from big windows with a spectacular view of Manhattan, the elegant minimalist interior design, and the calm of the various work groups in their connecting spaces. In the summer of 2012, there were about seventy "Shiners" as Cheni Yerushalmi calls them. Yerushalmi is a co-founder of Sunshine Suites, the company that manages this and two other co-working spaces in New York. Of the other two, one is in NoHo, and one in Tribeca. The Sunshine Bronx Business Incubator, however, is special because it received $250,000 from the city government in its effort to create an economic revival in the area. It hopes that here, too, new businesses will flower, especially in the new media and technology sectors.

Another reason it is special is because of the challenge it poses to stereotypes of the South Bronx. "I accepted Mayor Bloomberg's offer to open here because it is an extraordinary chance to create value in a place not known for the best things," explains Yerushalmi. "And the people who live in the Bronx understand that. They are used to the Manhattan community looking down on them, and this is their opportunity to give the talent that exists here as well as in Manhattan a chance to emerge. In fact, here in the Bronx, there is an abundance of a very important quality for entrepreneurs: to have suffered failure and gotten over it by adapting to the environment. People here have learned a lesson or two and thanks to word-of-mouth, new job seekers are arriving here daily, hoping to work for us."

Only six months after starting out, the first balance sheet is encouraging. Total billings for the Bronx incubator have reached half a million dollars and continue to grow. About half of the companies are high-tech, such as Miguel Sanchez's Mass Ideation, a digital design and 3D animation startup, whose clients include important brands such as Belvedere Vodka. Another is Think Work Media, a digital advertising agency founded by Shayne Spencer and also Yadilka, a design company that does marketing and creates websites. It was created by Yadilka Frias, a 27-year-old who was born in the Dominican Republic as many of the inhabitants of the South Bronx. "I live with my boyfriend and my one-year-old son fifteen minutes from here," says Yadilka. "I like Sunshine because it's so much more than a work space, it's a community where you can learn to grow, and form alliances with others to find customers."[3]

"Most of the people who work here live in the Bronx, but

it's not a requirement," points out Yerushalmi. "For example, Shayne commutes from Brooklyn. We're open to everyone. The diversity of activities in the incubator is important because ideas and businesses grow out of working together. An external investigation company does the only real selection process, to avoid having dangerous types in our midst, such as ex-cons who committed serious crimes. It is an absolute necessity to guarantee the safety of both the physical and intellectual property of our clients." So far as the risk of street crime is concerned, entry to the "fortress" is well guarded and the offices are not open at night or on weekends.

Fees are affordable. They start at $99 a month for a "virtual office" to $275 dollars for desk space, and go up to a $1,000 and more for a real ad-hoc office. A special feature is that renting space can be for just one month and there is a lot of flexibility in how one can rent space.

"Sunshine began in Manhattan in July 2001 because I needed a place to rent on a month-to-month basis," recalls Yerushalmi. "So I founded it with my best friend, Joe Raby. How it got its name is a funny story. Joe and I were in a club having a drink, and it was really late. We met a really cute girl, Sunshine, and her husband, who did IT installations. The next morning our lawyer called us and told us that the company had to be registered and so it needed a name. I was totally hung over and had a terrible headache, so Joe suggested calling the company Sunshine. It didn't seem like a good idea to me; our office was in Chelsea and I didn't like the sound of us being called the 'Sunshine Boys' ... but I was too tired to argue. And later on Sunshine's husband became our IT tech person."

"Nothing ever goes as planned," observes Yerushalmi, a 40-year-old who lives with his girlfriend and two dogs. "I'm an Israeli and I immigrated to the U. S. with my family when I was eleven. I didn't want to come, but my brother was ill and he could only be treated in New York. The first friend I made here was Joe, an Iraqi, and since then we have always been close. I was shy and didn't do well at school; I attended three colleges over a six-year period and never managed to graduate. Now universities ask me to lecture to their students. Over the years thousands of people have passed through Sunshine Suites and some of them have become famous, like Gary Vaynerchuck, author of the bestseller *The Thank You Economy*. Gary now gets paid $30,000 per speaking engagement."

Transparency, honesty, and values—these are the words Yerushalmi constantly uses, fixing you with his blue eyes and guru-look, an appearance he accentuates with the pearl bracelets and silver rings he wears. "I believe in the concept of communal work and to tell the truth, it's part of my history," he explains. "My father Yossi was a lawyer in Israel and was a strong supporter of the kibbutz philosophy. He took on what appeared to be a losing battle against the banks that wanted to repossess the land his kibbutz was built on, and he won. People were very proud of him. I was just a young child and didn't understand. But later I realized how important that community he was fighting for was. Every member of the community was ready and willing to help at the same level. And that is my inspiration for Sunshine's open model."

One more look at the high-tech future of the Bronx reveals yet another surprising view of the area. From the bathrooms at Sunshine you can see the cloisters of the monastery of the Dominican nuns of Corpus Christi. It has been there for over one hundred years, an island of tranquility and spirituality that miraculously survived the ruin of the 70s and 80s. And if the nuns could survive, why not believe in the miracle of the "Shiners"?

9
The 3D Generation
Long Island City in Queens

Long Island City holds the record for playing host to the largest dot-com to have successfully survived the burst of the bubble in 2000. This was none other than FreshDirect.com, an e-commerce company in the food sector, studied and imitated by so many on both sides of the Atlantic. Since 2012, Long Island City has also become one of the world centers for a new way to mass-produce goods using 3D printers. Shapeways, the startup that wants to "make things possible, easy and inexpensive, and manufacture any object created by anyone for whomever" has opened a factory here.

Long Island City is located on the East River and bounded by Astoria on the north, and Greenpoint in Brooklyn on the south. But this part of Queens still has a long way to go before becoming another center of New York high-tech. It doesn't have the "cool factor" of the fashion industry or the "hip factor" of the avant-garde, or so say the real estate brokers who are nevertheless doing everything they can to promote it. Office rents here are only $15 to $25 a square foot, compared to the $30/sq. ft. in Dumbo, the $40 in Chelsea or the $56 in the Flatiron area. Long Island City also has its art galleries and interesting museums such as Isamu Noguchi's or the Socrates Sculpture Park. And the riverfront is being renewed with parks and new apartment buildings. Another but no less important reason that attracts business are the tax breaks offered by the city of New York to those willing to set up shop here. Shapeways has accepted the offer.

There is a great deal of tough competition among local city councils to attract business and jobs. FreshDirect.com managed to set off a bidding war between New Jersey and New York to see who would offer more to play host to its new 495,000 square foot headquarters, almost 200,000 square feet bigger than their current office space. The Bronx won with an incentive package of $120 million between tax breaks and cash paid for by the Bronx borough, the city of New York, and the state of New York. And so FreshDirect.com will move to the Bronx as soon as its new headquarters in the Harlem River Yard are ready.

Long Island City is looking ahead and hopes that new entrepreneurs will be coming its way, possibly connected to the start of construction of the Cornell NYC Tech campus on Roosevelt Island in 2014. The new campus is located directly opposite this bank of the river. In the meantime, one of the local companies, Plaxal, up to now involved in the printing of plastic materials, has recycled itself as a real estate operation offering its services to technological startups. It has asked for public money to transform its Hunters Point (Long Island City) industrial building into an incubator, and has also begun to rent out office space in another of its buildings to companies such as Digital Natives Group, an educational startup.[1] In addition, it is also one of the major sponsors of the Queens Tech Meetup network, created in the spring of 2012 and with a membership that already numbers over 500.[2]

Today FreshDirect.com employs 2,200 people, it has 600,000 customers and, according to estimates by its co-founder and

CEO Jason Ackerman, it has generated one billion dollar of economic activity in New York State based on its payroll and purchasing history since 2002, the year it launched its online supermarket. The company was founded in 1999, in the middle of the Internet bubble, but Ackerman, who was then a 32-year-old investment banker specializing in the food sector, and his partner Joe Fedele, a fifty-year-old in the fresh food business, managed not to make the same mistakes as the first online supermarkets like Webvan. Webvan went bust two years after raising $1.2 billion with its 1999 IPO.

Ackerman and Fedele gave a lot of thought to a new model, and it took them over two years to put it into practice. They cut out the middlemen in the food chain, and were able to reach the consumer directly with an extremely competitive quality-price ratio. Their secret is to buy the food directly from the producer, process it—for example, smoke the salmon, butcher the meat, roast the coffee beans, bake breads and cakes— package it in made-to-measure portions for each customer, in accordance with their requests, and finally, deliver it to the home for a six dollar fee for a minimum thirty dollar purchase. Their web site is principally an interactive guide to how to do your shopping and it entices users to buy more. Based on its customers' tastes, it makes suggestions on how to choose and prepare the ingredients; it recommends seasonal or local foodstuffs, health foods, and also many prepared dishes made by FreshDirect chefs. These factors account for why its profit margins are higher than those of traditional supermarkets, and why the company has shown a profit since 2004.

It is a success story that the British supermarket chain WM Morrison decided to study in order to replicate it in Britain, which is why they bought a ten percent stake in FreshDirect for $50 million in March 2011. And since May of that same year, after various changes at the top, as well as in the organizational structure of the company, Ackerman has become the CEO. His uncle, Peter Ackerman, an ex-Wall Street banker, was FreshDirect's first investor, putting in $65 million. Jason's mission now is to transform FreshDirect from a local to a national company, something like an Amazon.com of the food sector offering fruit and vegetables, meat and fish, and cheese and deli products instead of books and DVDs.[3]

Plastic and ceramics, steel and silver, nylon and glass are just a few examples of the thirty different materials used at Shapeways to manufacture over 100,000 objects a month with its 3D printers. "It is a technology that is destined to revolutionize industry," says Peter Weijmarshausen, co-founder and CEO. "Within the next ten years, ten percent of world production will no longer be mass production; instead it will be personalized."

Born in the Netherlands 41 years ago, with a degree in applied physics from the Eindhoven University of Technology, Weijmarshausen began working with Linux open source software in 1991 and two years later he and a team from his company NaN, which stands for "Not a Number," used it to create Blender, a free 3D graphics and modeling program. In 2007 he got the chance to work in the Philips Lifestyle Incubator (PLI) in Eindhoven on a 3D printer project. A year later, Shapeways was created and in 2010 it left the incubator.

Shapeways "helps make and sell things," from really small items as a ring, to much larger ones as a chair. The company offers 3D software to design them, the hardware needed to make them, and a virtual store to sell them from. The site users range from hobbyists to about fifteen hundred professional designers worldwide, and the site also hosts about six thousand "shops." There are just a few days between the glimmer of an idea for a product to its "printing" and online sales and during this period, Shapeways, using its software, verifies the technical feasibility of the object, prices it, and proceeds to realization. Shapeways' profit margin is calculated into the price. "In only four days, a friend of mine managed to make and sell hundreds of cases for the first iPads right after they came on the market," says Weijmarshausen. At the end of 2010 besides the offices in Holland, he decided to open a second office near the Flatiron District in New York. "We realized that many of our customers and designers were in the U.S.," explains Weijmarshausen. "And in addition, it was more difficult to find new financing in Europe for our development, especially after the economic crisis of 2008." So far, Union Square Ventures in the U.S. and Index Ventures in London have together invested $17.3 million in Shapeways.

So the new Long Island City factory, with 20 employees, joins the Dutch factory that produced 100,000 objects a month in 2012. "We are hoping to reach three to four million pieces a month," says Weijmarshausen, who is pleased by his New York welcome. "The mindset here is ideal for a technological startup. Agreements on deals and projects are reached quickly. Angel investors and venture capitalists provide capital and good advice. It's easy to meet interesting people who understand the business, design and high-tech. And everyone works together with an open spirit."[4]

10

Meucci's Phone: A Failed Startup

Lessons from Staten Island

Superstorm Sandy's scars will be visible for a long time on Staten Island, the New York borough hardest-hit by the disaster that took place on October 29, 2012. Its residents call it "the forgotten borough" ignored both by local politicians and the city council. Most other New Yorkers have never been to Staten Island, with its population of less than half a million, one third of whom are of Italian origin. And if tourists do go there, it is only to take advantage of the fantastic views from the ferry that links it to Manhattan. Often, as soon as they reach the Staten Island side, they go right back to Manhattan. As a result, it's not surprising to learn that Staten Island barely exists on the digital map of New York. It's too "uncool." It has no appeal for the young people who are at the core of the metropolitan startups.

Yet included in the education of someone who wants to create a startup should be a mandatory visit to the museum-home of Antonio Meucci, the largely unknown Italian inventor of the most revolutionary means of communication prior to the Internet: the telephone. It is a modest house halfway between the pier where the Staten Island ferry docks and the Verrazano Bridge. Ironically, it is better known as the place where

Giuseppe Garibaldi, the "hero of two worlds," stayed for a few years, rather than the laboratory where Meucci worked on his invention.[1] Visiting it and hearing the unfortunate story of its tenant, is an important lesson in how not to create a startup. Even with an ingenious idea, one can be a failure without an adequate business plan and the necessary capital.

In 1850, Meucci, an Italian-born engineer from Florence, decided to seek his fortune in New York, feeling that it was the right place to continue his research and transform it into a business. His intuition was good, but the Italian immigrant, who was 42 at the time, didn't know a word of English, and so chose what seemed to be the easiest route to start his life in the city. He took up residence in what, at the time, was the largest Italian community in New York: Staten Island. The problem was that Meucci was unable to make the necessary cultural leap to link up to the American business community that could have financed him. He never became fluent in English and the first demo of his invention, the "telectrophone" was held in 1860 before an all-Italian audience. As a result, the only New York newspaper that covered the invention was the Italian language *L'Eco d'Italia*.

Wall Street and the venture capitalists of the time were a long way away and totally in the dark regarding the fight for survival of Meucci's startup, the Telettrofono Company, that he had founded in 1871 with three other Italians, Angelo Zilio Grandi, Angelo Antonio Tremeschin, and Sereno Breguglia Tremeschin. It seems incredible today, but Meucci couldn't even raise the $250 required for the legal work to submit the patent; consequently he only got a temporary registration, a preliminary step to getting a real patent that cost $20 and expired after one year.

From that beginning, the story of the "telectrophone" was a succession of misfortunes. Several of Meucci's prototypes were lost by the Western Union Telegraph Company of New York—

Meucci had turned to them in order to have an industrial test run on his invention. His wife, in dire straights while Meucci was ill in the hospital, sold the others. The temporary patent he had registered cost $10 each time it had to be renewed, and Meucci gave it up in 1874. Moreover, the legal documentation had been drawn up badly by a low-cost lawyer. Two years later, in 1876, the patent for the invention of the telephone was awarded to Alexander Graham Bell, who, quite differently, had the good fortune of having two strong investors and business partners, Gardiner Hubbard and Thomas Sanders, co-founders of the Bell Telephone Company.

With his own startup a failure, and unable to defend himself in court as the inventor of the "telectrophone," Meucci died a poor, broken man. To make matters worse, there were those who accused him of trying to scam investors. It was only in 2002, thanks to the work of the Staten Island congressman Vito Fossella, that the U.S. House of Representatives approved a resolution recognizing the "extraordinary and tragic career of the great Italian inventor," establishing the fact that the patent for the telephone would have been his, had he had the money to cut through the red tape.[2]

This sad history offers the first lesson for those who would contemplate a startup today: get the best possible legal representation. The second lesson: get out of your comfort zone. And the third: speak really good English!

The New York City Economic Development Corporation intends to open a startup technology incubator on Staten Island. In the fall of 2012, it asked for projects to be submitted for consideration and these submissions are now under evaluation. If the venture goes ahead, it will be a small but meaningful step toward the recovery of Staten Island after the terrible beating inflicted by Sandy.

III

Themes

On the Present and the Future of New York

11

A Kinder, Gentler City

How Was the NY Community Created?

"I could have never done in Europe what I have accomplished here, and that's an amazing achievement for New York City," says Boštjan Špetič, the Slovenian founder and CEO of Zemanta. "I talked to people who started companies before 2007. All of them were committed to making New York a great startup city. They were focused on their startups and on making New York an awesome city to start companies in. There are investors like Fred Wilson who have that vision, and NYCEDC is very active. I don't know how they found out about me, but they reached out to me after a few months to get to know me and understand what I was doing. They sent me an email saying: 'Hi, can we schedule a meeting so that we can get to know each other and see what your needs are?' That was fantastic. I got the impression that somebody was doing something right, either by incentivizing or just by being welcoming. I felt that joining this current was the right thing to do, so I promote New York when I talk to Europeans now."

Špetič's testimony reveals how much New York has evolved as an ecosystem favorable to startups. Many other regions in America and in the rest of the world are seeking to become successful entrepreneurial centers, especially in the high-tech sector. But what are the right ways to reach this goal?

Brad Feld, partner and co-founder of Foundry Group, a venture capital firm in Boulder, Colorado, wrote a book on the topic.[1] An indispensable element is the presence of excellent universities, and it's a plus to have incentives from the local administration, but the difference then comes from the "character" of the place, and the generations of entrepreneurs who reinvest the fruits of their successes into new startups, whether their own or of others.

"The finest intentions and best laid plans don't always produce results without that elusive 'something else' that must fall into place," observes Don Katz, founder and CEO of Audible, headquartered in Newark, New Jersey. "I am very focused on trying to help Newark come back from years and years of deprivation," says Katz. "Newark was one of the richest cities in the world, because it had a great harbor, and was the home of successful businesses such as Ballantine, one of the oldest brands of beer in the United States. Then it hit really hard times. Audible moved in here, because I thought that with all the transportation advantages and the charisma of mayor Cory Booker, we would be part of a movement. It has not really happened. I am on the economic development board of the city, and I am really interested in figuring out how you can lay out what people need to start these businesses. Because it is always different: Silicon Valley is very formulaic as to what happened there, with the university, the original scale companies and the character of the engineer/entrepreneur that would break off. But I am intrigued by what is the secret sauce at this point, because there is no real great reason why Vinegar Hill in Brooklyn becomes a startup area except that there's plenty of skinny jeans stores and pork pie hats stores, but it has bad bandwidth and bad space. And what about Detroit 2.0? It has become a really interesting phenomenon: Josh Linkner, the founder of ePrize, has a venture fund and has moved downtown; Dan Gilbert, the founder of Quicken Loans bought seven square blocks and moved there, and together with Compuserve has created a whole new tech development center. That was because Dan got pissed off when he found out that the Groupon guys were from Detroit and they moved to Chicago. It was not like they went to Palo Alto!"

New York is now on its second or third generation of startups and has a good fabric of local entrepreneurs, managers and investors. Fred Wilson, co-founder and managing partner of Union Square Ventures, describes the current situation compared to the '90s: "There are a lot more angel investments, and there are a lot more people who have worked in one or more startups. It's not just the serial entrepreneurs who have started their fourth or fifth companies; it's also about all the team members who started with them in company number one and who have joined them as co-founders in company two, or who have joined the team of a following company. Some people can't or don't want to be founders, but they can be the consumer service agents in company number one, and then the marketing directors in company number two, and the COOs in company number three. There are a lot of people like that."

"If you look at startup hubs," Wilson continues, "Silicon Valley being the biggest and best of those, and you look back at the '60s, you had a few companies, Intel and maybe a few other semiconductor companies. From their success and from the wealth that was made in those companies, some people never started a company; some people became angel investors; some people became venture capitalists, and some employees in those companies made enough money to start their next companies. So, there was the wave of companies such as Cisco, Oracle and Apple. Then, the next wave was companies like Netscape. Then, the next wave was companies like Google and Yahoo! Then, the next wave was companies such as Facebook and Twitter. Each one of these waves is bigger and bigger because the amount of wealth created in the previous wave becomes the capital foundation for the next wave. And the amount of talent that was created in the previous wave forms the talent for the next wave."

"If you think about it this way," adds Wilson, "New York had its first wave from 1994 to 2000. There were some companies that got created then. Not all of them were successful. Some survived, and some got bought. But from there, we had the next wave that created a bunch of companies, and now we're almost in the third wave. A lot of venture capital came out of those successes. For example Kevin Ryan, who was the second CEO of DoubleClick, went on to create Gilt Groupe, Business Insider and 10gen. He is now running one of these companies (Gilt Groupe), and he has invested in all of them. There are dozens of such stories. That's what's different this time: it's a more developed economy. And the success of this wave will lead to the success of the next one."

Ryan recalls New York in 1996, when he became CEO of DoubleClick: "There were hardly any venture capital firms that really invested in startup companies. Almost none of our first hundred employees at DoubleClick had ever worked for a startup. There were just no startups. I couldn't even find a lawyer in New York to take our company public because they were all on the West Coast. Today, the infrastructure is completely different. There is an angel network; there are many VC firms; VC firms that were located in Boston and San Francisco are now hiring partners in New York because it's the most promising area. On *Business Insider* there is a good article about the 12 private companies in New York that are worth more than $500 million. Four years ago that number was one. That is what's really emerging: we've had more success stories."

"Nothing works like success," agrees angel investor Chris Dixon, and he stresses that New York needs more successful companies: "It says to the rest of the world that this is the place to be, and it says to New Yorkers that this is the way you can be successful. I tried to do what I can to make that happen, whether by starting companies or investing in other people's companies. I also blog and do other things. That kind of marketing, just getting the message out that there are people here, is also important. What we do have now and didn't have before, are a lot of serious investors, people who have experience in the field and who are able to advise entrepreneurs."

The willingness of industry leaders to promote the technological community, and to act as mentors to new generations of entrepreneurs is an important component for the development of a startup community. And New York is committed to this. "I'm a second generation tech entrepreneur, and I spend some of my time trying to give back to the tech scene," says Dennis Crowley, co-founder and CEO of Foursquare. "I try to answer questions that people might have about how to get started here. I'm doing that because, when we were doing DodgeBall (Crowley's previous startup) we didn't have anyone to ask. We didn't know anyone on the scene. There was no one to make connections for us. I'm pretty easy to find online, and my attitude is: if there's anything I can do to help you guys out, let me know. I can make introductions for you to other companies, to people in our company, to investors or whatever you need to get you from where you are to the next step. I'm happy to make these connections with people. We really struggled to get Dodgeball off the ground, and I think it's awesome we ended up at Google [as an acquisition] because it kick-started a lot of the stuff we're doing now. But we got lucky on the way, and I want to help people go through the same experience as we did."

Crowley, Dixon, Ryan, Wilson and many other entrepreneurs and successful investors don't get tired of attending conferences and mentoring programs to share their experiences and collaborate in the creation of new startups. There are many facilities that host these initiatives in New York, from simple co-working spaces to incubators or accelerators. "Incubators, accelerators, masturbators!" jokes angel investor Brian Cohen. "They're all looking for some orgasmic final hit. But they serve a purpose. They pose an opportunity for all these entrepreneurs to share and to listen to one another. They also provide a place for mentorship to happen. With all these companies out there, they allow some screening to take place too, which a lot of angel investors have neither the time, nor the money, nor the inclination for. They provide the early stage of screening. Plus, if the light is shining on them, the money is shining on them too. So they're good, and they'll continue to grow. Commercial businesses, big businesses such as Bloomberg L.P. and BMW are also developing them in New York as their R&D labs."

But what was the spark that got technology started in New York? Trust is the real asset of New York according to Cohen: "I can't think of a specific company. I can't think of a specific individual. I can't think of any specific deal. I can't think of any specific situation. I'd say it's a sense of camaraderie that started the tech community in New York. I've never seen more trust. If somebody told me that there are a lot of people with a lot of money here, and that they all work together and trust each other, I would never have believed it. When there's so much money to be made, you can't imagine that there are enough people out there to trust each other. But New York City has this trust. I'm amazed. I'm putting together a list right now to meet guys from the Technion, the Israeli university that with Cornell will build the new campus, and I asked friends of mine to give me names of people I should invite. Everybody is inviting everybody! There's a real psychology of inclusion rather than exclusion going on. I can call anyone not because I'm a member of charities or of an angel group, but because everybody is ready to listen."

12
Alley versus Valley
How Is New York Different from Other Entrepreneurial Hubs?

New York was founded by Dutch merchants. Making money with commerce is part of its DNA. It has a practical spirit, different from the "California dreamers" that drove the first gold prospectors and other waves of pioneers to migrate to the Golden State. This historical and psychological difference is also reflected in the way of doing business today in the tech sector, and it's not a disadvantage for the Big Apple with respect to Silicon Valley. Rather, it is a strong point in this new phase of the Internet.

Fred Wilson sums up the difference in mentality: "The technology business as it's done here in New York is a peer to the other industries in the city; the technology business as it's done in Silicon Valley is a thing on its own. The business is more commercial here in New York. People who are in it want to make money, whereas people in the technology business in California say that they're in it to change the world. I think that's healthy at some level, but I don't think it's healthy at an absolute level. People should be in business to make money. In New York that kind of commercialism is part of the scene. People understand that they need to have revenues and profits and that kind of stuff. A lot of the entrepreneurs here in New York are entrepreneurs, not engineers. A lot of entrepreneurs in Silicon Valley are engineers who have built something and have found themselves in business, not the other way around. Entrepreneurs in New York can figure out how to build things, but they're business people first; and they tend to be more industry-focused. You see things as retail-tech and fashion-tech and art-tech and consumer finance-tech, and all those things inspired by the large industries that are centered here in New York. That's one factor. Companies are less core-technology driven and more focused on the application of technologies. It doesn't mean that they're not tech companies, in fact they have a lot of software engineers, but they're not typically building the infrastructure. They tend to take technology and apply it to more commercial problems."

More business oriented than their West Coast counterparts, New York entrepreneurs are also more careful with money, which in the long run could be healthier. "My thinking," says Brian Cohen, "is that a lot of companies on the East Coast have been underfunded, and a lot of companies on the West Coast are funded in a way that money is not a problem for them. Silicon Valley tends to hire Alpha males—'we'll win the war at all costs.' Here, we're more creative types, we'll figure it out. There, it's like 'How much did you say you needed? Two million dollars? Would you do better if I gave you one more million?' And they get it. All of a sudden, money is not an issue anymore. In a marketplace that is defined by hiring the best, the finest, money talks. The best have to have incentives to work there. Sure, they get more money than what they need, but the valuations are higher, and that works out. Here in New York,

I'm beginning to see an approach that goes 'I'll get you enough to get to that point. Let's keep the valuation lower, right?' In New York, it's about giving you enough money to get to your milestone. There is more money in California, and there is more ease in giving it. In New York, there's a lot of money, but there's a different psychology. I'll fund you: how much money do you need? Can you do it for less? In California, they'll never ask you that question."

New opportunities for New York as a high-tech hub are related to the evolution of the Internet, according to Chris Dixon: "Imagine the Internet as a house. The first phase— laying the foundation, the bricks—happened in the '90s. No wonder that Boston and California, heavy tech places with MIT and Stanford, dominated the scene at that time. The house has been built, now it's more about interior design. Many interesting, recent companies haven't been started by technologists but by design and product-oriented people, which has helped New York a lot. New York City has always been a consumer media kind of city, and the Internet is in need of those kinds of skills now. Actually, when I say design, it's more about product-focused people. I'd put Facebook in that category. Everything requires engineers, but unlike Google, their breakthrough was not as scientific. It was a well-designed product that people liked to use. Google had a significant scientific breakthrough with their search algorithm. That's not what drives Facebook. In *The Social Network* movie, when they write equations on the wall that's just not what it is, it's not about that. Every company has engineering problems, but Facebook is product-design driven."

Algorithms do not dominate the current phase of the Internet, explains Tristan Louis, a French-American Internet veteran, founder and CEO of Keepskor. "If you look at it in historic terms, the technology field was traditionally dominated by algorithms," Louis wrote on his blog.[1] "Hardware and software solutions in the past meant that people were not as essential to success in technology. As the web became more social, cultural anthropology has become more essential. It is no wonder that none of the major new players in the tech field has come out of the Valley in the last five years. Flickr was born in Canada, Skype in Europe, Facebook in Boston, Twitter and Zynga in San Francisco (according to Wikipedia, SF is not part of Silicon Valley), Groupon in Chicago, and Foursquare and bit.ly came from New York. This is not to discount the value of algorithmic approaches. Companies that are depending on heavy math and engineering will continue to thrive in the valley (I'm thinking of companies such as Google, Netflix and Apple, for example). But those will have to reach out to talent in the cities if they want to thrive in the social web (interestingly enough, it seems that Facebook and Google have now started to realize this as they are poaching New York startups or expanding their physical footprint in the city in an attempt to get social DNA flowing back into their companies)."

Kevin Ryan agrees that today, in certain areas of the Internet space, Silicon Valley is not particularly relevant: "Look at flash sales, for example. There are probably eight large flash sales companies. Four of them are in New York, Gilt Groupe, Ideeli, Lot18 and Fab.com. San Francisco has one, Boston has one, Los Angeles has one, and Seattle has one. In the ad technology space, San Francisco is not really that relevant. DoubleClick was by far the biggest company, the next biggest ones were 24/7 and aQuantive. DoubleClick and 24/7 were here, and aQuantive was in Seattle. RealMedia was in New York, too. I don't think there was one in San Francisco. I was on the board of iJobs, GroupBuilder's competitor based in New York. They were not in San Francisco. Dice is in New York, Indeed is in New York, The Ladders is in New York. The Internet is not one sector; there really are 12 sub-sectors."

"The creative world in New York has become extremely helpful as user experience has become essential for every company," adds angel investor David Tisch. Whether it's the design schools, whether it's programs such as ITP) at NYU, or Parsons, or the digital agencies, the fact that New York is so design-centric has been extremely valuable to the startup scene here. The majority of startups here in New York are innovating in different ways using technology to disrupt businesses, or technology as an enabler, and they are built on other things. If you're in certain businesses, you should come and build your company here. If you're in the advertisement, financial technology, fashion, sports, media or publishing industry, even in education, you have to be in New York."

Tisch points out two other important characteristics of New York: population density and cultural diversity. "If you're a company that is dependent on population density, you have to be here," Tisch says. "It's not only the consumer population; it's also business population density. There are more small businesses per square mile in New York than anywhere else in the world. Companies like Foursquare should be based here because they can figure out how to scale. The same is true for SeamlessWeb and FreshDirect. If you make it in New York, a) you might not have to go anywhere else, b) if you figured out how to scale New York, you can go anywhere. Moreover, what is great about New York is that there is so much else besides tech going on. You are exposed to people from all walks of life, and from so many different industries. If you mention the fact that you're in a tech startup during a party, people will still think that you're unemployed. They don't know about this tech scene in New York yet, and that's extremely healthy. Another thing is: if you're beta testing a product, you can get on the subway, and every single subway stop is a distinctive set of demographics to test your product with. Where else in the world can you do that? If you just ride around on the subway, you can test your product on so many different people, with so many diverse backgrounds, jobs and interests. That's totally unique to New York. It's the craziest and most varied environment in the world, and that helps companies a lot. People come here striving to be the best at whatever it is they're doing, and that's not any different for technology, everyone here wants to be the best. I think that creates a drive in companies here to really win."

13

A Cool Place to Live
What Makes New York Attractive?

"The fact is, every city creates its own future. If you believe you're at the mercy of larger forces beyond your control, you've already lost. Those larger forces affect every city, but successful cities learn how to adapt. New York learned that the hard way in the 1970s. Some of the lessons from that era now seem obvious: you can't borrow to meet operating expenses. You can't ignore petty criminals who breed a sense of lawlessness. You can't let housing abandonment destroy neighborhoods. You can't let the public school system become something that the middle class is afraid of. You can't drive the biggest taxpayers out of the city, thus increasing the burden on everyone else. And you can't allow quality of life to suffer, and that means keeping the parks clean, the subways safe and reliable, and the hospitals in good shape. These lessons may be obvious enough, but getting elected officials to apply them successfully is not so easy in part because politics and special interests always get in the way." Thus remarked Mayor Michael Bloomberg in a speech to the Economic Club of New York in March, 2009.[1]

Will these lessons be forgotten by whomever succeeds Bloomberg as mayor on Jan. 1, 2014? Possibly. Any success cannot be taken for granted. As early as 2012, amid controversy and legal challenges to the "stop and frisk" policy that gave New York police the right to stop and search "suspicious" characters, the rate of certain crimes (excluding murders) started to rise after hitting historical lows (+8.5% aggression without weapons and +3.4% those with arms, +9.4% serious thefts and +5.5% minor ones, +4.4% rapes and +11.8% minor sexual offenses, according to statistics of the New York Police Department for the first nine months of 2012 compared to the same period of the previous year)[2].

This is a warning signal that should not be underestimated. But the general trend over the last 20 years has been a general improvement of the quality of life in the Big Apple. "New York has just become more livable and cooler," says Kevin Ryan. "One of the things we've found at 10gen that is interesting is that we often give a choice to engineers who come out of college. 'Look, you're great, we'll make you an offer: you can work out of our San Francisco office, or you can work in New York.' Two thirds of them choose to live in New York because New York is a great, cool place." Chris Dixon agrees: "New York is a great place to live, a city where intellectual capital wants to go. That means low crime, interesting cultural stuff. That's the most important thing in my opinion."

Why didn't New York venture capitalists move to Silicon Valley, even when the majority of their investments were in California, and New York offered few business opportunities? Why did they prefer commuting between the two coasts for years? Fred Wilson's response gives a voice to many: "My wife Joanne and I were and still are really happy here in New York. The thing that is interesting about New York is that you have a social life that's diverse. Joanne has had several careers. Her first career was in the fashion business, so she had all sorts of friends from the apparel and fashion business. She also had friends from Wall Street, from the media industry and so on and so forth. We've always liked that, and we've always been nervous about moving to California, because we thought it would be very one-dimensional. Everybody we would know and see in California would be from the technology business. There's nothing wrong with the technology business—that's the business I've been in my entire life—but we were nervous that we would be giving up this diverse, fun group of people for a more one-dimensional group. I've always been really excited to live in New York."

"There's another thing about New York: the bar scene and the restaurant scene for the 'kids,'" adds Brian Cohen. "There's no better place to hang out than in New York. The city's environment is so much more conducive to that. You can't do that in Silicon Valley. You can't walk from San Mateo to Mountain View, you know? If you're in the city, you may go to 12 different bars, hang out with 40 different friends … it's another matter. I think the real catalyst is that New York is totally walkable, you can walk anywhere, and every place is safe. Where would you go to live this life? Nowhere." But even Cohen is worried about the after-Bloomberg: "There's no businessman who could fit in his shoes. I think New York is going to go through a difficult time then. He's had an impact in ways people have no understanding of. That will be gone."

But the answer to the feared "return to the past" is in the "New York state of mind," as Fred Wilson describes it, discussing the impact of the City on a friend who had recently moved from San Francisco: "He told me he was taken with the hyperactivity of New Yorkers. I asked him where he thought it comes from. He had a great answer. He said that New York is 'meta-unstable' meaning that it is inherently unstable and therefore in a constant state of implosion. And New Yorkers implicitly understand that. So the only way we can keep the city functioning is to be constantly seeking to upgrade it in real time. So that's why the city is in a constant state of construction. That's why New Yorkers are always looking for a better way to do something and a faster way to get somewhere. This may sound like psycho physics babble. In fact it is. But it also captures something inherent in the NYC psychology that I have felt since the day I arrived here in 1983. This city is in a constant state of seeking to get to a better place. And that is why it is such a great place to be an entrepreneur—despite all the challenges of operating a business in NYC. And it is why I felt at home here the day I arrived, and why I suspect I always will."[3]

14

City of Women

Is New York a Hospitable Place for Female Entrepreneurs?

"New York has a more conducive climate to high-tech women entrepreneurs compared to other cities: startups founded by women here are twice that in Silicon Valley or in London, as a percent of the total." This statement is from Rachel Sterne Haot, the chief digital officer (CDO) of New York City, at the first NY Tech Meetup dedicated to the presentation of companies founded or led by women. Eight enterprises "walked the runway" that evening, June 14, 2012, at the headquarters of Microsoft in Midtown Manhattan: Fathom, The Mission List, HonestlyNow, ElectNext, VenueBook, Paperlex, Prone, and Findings.

Sterne Haot cited research by "Startup Genome" on the characteristics of the ecosystems where most startups are created. An interesting fact is the gender of the founders. Out of 100 New York new high-tech companies, 20 are founded by women and 80 by men only; in Silicon Valley and London the ratio drops to 10-90.

Before her appointment as CDO by New York Mayor

Michael Bloomberg in January 2011, Sterne Haot, 28 years old, had created two startups herself: the "citizen journalism" site GroundReport with seven thousand contributors from around the world (2006); and the digital consulting firm Upward (2009).

Many factors explain the gentle touch of a city that, according to the stereotypes, ought to be harsh and inhospitable, in particular for women and children. From a business standpoint, New York is the capital of American fashion and media, industries where women have been typically to establish themselves more easily. And from a practical point of view, it is less complicated to balance work and family in a place where you can walk between home and office, have the groceries delivered, and enjoy excellent services of all kinds just a click or phone call away.

But that is not to say that New York is the "perfect" paradise for women entrepreneurs.

The percentage of women who manage to get into startup programs and get funding from investors is not near its full potential, as many members of New York's tech community are quick to affirm. For this reason, three of them, Veronika Sonsev (founder and CEO of inSparq), Deborah Jackson (founder and CEO of JumpThru), and Kelley Hoey, consultant and connector par excellence, have created the first accelerator and mentoring program dedicated to startups conceived and led by women (alone or with men as partners): Women Innovate Mobile (WIM), specializing in technologies and applications for mobile devices.

The first edition of the program took place between late March and late June, 2012, with the participation of 12 startups. The best of them then participated in a glamorous "demo day" event in Tribeca that resembled a fashion show. The setting was the penthouse of Barry Appelman, the inventor of, among other things, AOL instant messaging, with special guest Alexandra Wilkis Wilson, co-founder of Gilt Groupe and author of a book on how Gilt was built.[1] "There are still not enough women who start large companies, and this is an initiative to encourage them," said Wilkis Wilson, 35 and mother of a two-year old child.

"A problem is the bias that still exists among investors to always bet on the same type of startup, founded and managed by men," said angel investor Jerry Neumann, who attended the WIM demo day with his daughter, Lea.

Sonsev is a realist, and asked whether venture capitalists and angel investors have a bias in favor of male company founders she responds: "If you are at a party and you look for somebody to talk to about tech business, you will look for a guy with a hoodie—the next Zuckerberg. It's a natural bias." At the same time she defends the idea of having created an accelerator just for women: "Other accelerators are effective, but less than 10% of participating startups have women as founders or co-founders. If a group is exclusively male, the culture is male and it might not be a nice environment: women are not encouraged to get into it. When I joined AOL in '98 I was the first professional woman in my division (prior to me joining there were only secretaries) and when I arrived my boss asked the other guys to stop cursing, for example. Before me it was different, of course. Having said that, I never felt that I was a victim of discrimination."

WIM is without a doubt a success for the interest it generated: "Because our accelerator is seen as friendly to women founders, we have received 139 applications from all over the US and the world, including companies from Canada, India, and Israel. And thanks to our initiative, I think, TechStars, in its last program, had an increase in the number of startups with women founders," explains Sonsev, who was born in Russia in 1975, and emigrated four years later to America with her family.

She studied economics at the American University and, after 12 years in AOL, in 2010, founded inSparq, a social marketing and analytics platform for e-commerce sites.

Sonsev is single and for now does not intend to start a family: "I'm too passionate about building my own business," she explains. On the topic of reconciling kids and startups, opinions differ.

It is easier for a woman entrepreneur to manage her time according to her own needs, says Joanne Wilson, 51, married to venture capitalist Fred Wilson. She is an angel investor herself and author of the blog "Gotham Gal," where she often discusses the topic of family, along with the startups that she has invested in and that are mostly founded by women.

Wilson began as a manager and buyer for Macy's department store, and then as a business development executive in a New York textile company. Having witnessed firsthand the Internet bubble of 2000 (as number two and "moneymaker" of the *Silicon Alley Reporter* magazine founded by Jason Calacanis), Wilson then left work to raise three children. In October 2003, she started writing her blog with the idea of reconnecting to the technological community, but this activity also served to build her new career as an investor: in fact, contacts and business proposals usually arrive via email from her readers.

"Many times women's original ideas are filling voids in their lives," observes Wilson. "Women don't typically think of 'big tech' ideas. Zipcar was a woman's idea, and she probably came downstairs one day and thought 'Wouldn't it be great if I could just jump into a car and go?' And it ended up becoming a big business [and finally purchased by Avis]. Women are using technology as a platform and I think a lot of men might not understand their businesses. Once I heard some major venture capitalist say, 'I wish women would stop building these stupid fashion businesses ...' Really? I wish men would stop building these stupid tech businesses! I mean, you go where you are comfortable and that you understand, right?"

On the basis of her experience as an angel investor, having begun in 2007 by investing in the real estate news blog Curbed, Wilson believes that women founders of startups have special features: "First of all, they are in it for the long run; they are going to make sure they succeed at any level; they take money very seriously. And they all start to evolve as all businesses do. So, I think they are going to be more important going forward because women are the ones making all the purchases. And there are all these opportunities online for e-commerce businesses."

"I think everyone should be an entrepreneur because it allows you to have a certain lifestyle, particularly for women who have children and have lives that are constantly in flux," Wilson insists. "When you are an entrepreneur you own your own life. And to me if that means you have to go home at 3 o'clock because your kid is sick, you know you can do that. You have flexibility in your life because you are not reporting to anyone. When you are working in a small startup, like Buddy Media, that is about family and about having flexibility to do your job right in a non structured environment."

To young women who ask her "When should you have children?," Wilson replies: "It is not about the entrance strategy, it is about the exit strategy. Meaning you do not want to be 70 years old when your kids go off to college. It is never going to be perfect, so there's no reason to wait. My kids are going to be gone in a year and a half and I'm still young. If I had to do it all over again I would have done it even earlier, because you have to have energy to do new things and you can relate to your kids better because you are young too."

"If I were 10 years younger," Wilson adds, "I'd go out and raise a fund among wealthy families that believe in my mission, which is: changing the world through women entrepreneurs, so that we could help women grow their businesses and make a difference one person at a time. My goal is not to have returns of a hundred-fold: if someone is doing $20 million it's OK; if one of them got to $200 million, that's fantastic. Women should do startups because the only way to change environments that are relegated to a 9-5 day is if the changes come from outside corporate America. If every woman started a company and those companies ended up having market caps from $100K to $1 billion we would not only have changed the ratio, we would have changed the economy."

New York is not short of examples of women able to "bring up" children and startups, as told by *The New York Times* in a June 2012 report. There's Jennifer Fleiss, 28, who at the end of 2009 co-founded Rent the Runway, a site that rents dresses and accessories (with 2.5 million users) and who, at the end of 2011, became a mom.[2]

In the summer of 2010, Divya Gugnani, 35 years old, co-founded Send the Trend, an e-commerce site for accessories and beauty products (bought by QVC in February 2012), and in May 2012 had her first child. Carley Roney, 43 years old, who at the end of '99 had co-founded XO Group—now a public media company with a market capitalization of $300 million—has three children aged four to 14 years. Alexandra Wilkis Wilson and her friend Alexis Maybank, 37, are co-founders of Gilt Groupe and both have become mothers in 2010, two and a half years after the launch of the startup. All have always remained at the helm of their companies. But all waited to have children after launching the startup, except for Roney who, during the initial fundraising process, kept her baby "secret" for fear that the investors would believe motherhood would distract her from the business. Wilkis Wilson points out that timing is everything and that at the beginning of Gilt Groupe, when there were only eight employees, she could not have imagined caring for a child as well.

Even Cella Irvine, 54, CEO of Vibrant, a New York "contextual" online advertising agency, points out that most female startup founders are between 25 and 35 years old and have no children. Irvine is skeptical about the possibility of finding a balance between entrepreneurship and motherhood. She believes that the lifestyle of those who do the two things together is "the worst possible," though she has not lived this particular experience, having always been a company executive rather than a startup founder. In order to take care of her children—who are now 12 and 14, one male and one female—Irvine went on leave twice for a year, the first time when she was pregnant with her son and her daughter was almost three, and the second time when her kids were starting second and fourth grade.

"I did that specifically because, by that time, I had put work-life balance so far out of kilter that I felt I had to do something to change that," Irvine explains. "Since then, I have been much more mindful about trying to make sure that I set some boundaries."

Irvine wonders whether, behind the increased number of startups created by women, there isn't just a bad labor market and the difficulty of finding "normal" jobs. "There is a wave of startups right now that are focused on beauty and fashion, typically with an e-commerce angle, and many of them are started by well-dressed, sophisticated, highly educated women," says Irvine. "Now, I think it would be interesting to dig into why that is happening, including a view on how much of that stems from managing a poor employment environment, and how much of it really is a change in how comfortable women feel about being entrepreneurs."

But even if it were so, it would confirm women's ability to transform a problem into an opportunity.

15
Fail Cheap and Succeed Big
How Much Does It Take to Start a Company?

If you live in Manhattan, you know you can eat well because there are many small restaurants and there is high turnover; the bad ones close quickly. This is a metaphor often used by the former Wall Street trader Nassim Nicholas Taleb, now a philosopher and bestselling author of The Black Swan, in order to explain why the American financial system was better when there were many small banks and bankruptcies were more frequent. The system was more volatile, but also more robust. The metaphor also applies to the current new ecosystem of startups. They are many and small, and can experiment with new ideas and new technologies because the startup costs have dramatically decreased in recent years, and to fail is not a catastrophe. On the other hand, venture capitalists are risking pennies to earn many dollars, and they know how to take advantage of the positive side of Black Swans, those highly improbable, unexpected events that have a great impact, says Taleb. This is why venture capitalists are more robust than the big banks that risk many dollars to earn pennies: the former can collect billions bankrolling Black Swan Google; the latter can lose billions when a crisis erupts like that of subprime mortgages.[1]

Of course, even the venture capitalists suffered severe losses with the bursting of the Internet bubble in 2000. But since then, the system has evolved and strengthened to the benefit of both entrepreneurs and investors. A startup 15 years ago had to buy expensive servers and communications infrastructure, pay software licenses, and hire personnel to build and manage a data center, with minimum costs of $600,000 per year. Today, a startup can rely on infrastructure services provided by Amazon Web Services (or other providers), connect to "cloud computing," use Google's free software for office tasks, for a total of around $50,000 per year, according to a *Forbes* calculation.

"One of the differences that we have seen here is that it has become much less expensive to try things," confirms Howard Morgan. "When we started Infonautics in 1992, it cost us $5 million to make the first product. With Half.com in 2000 it only cost us $2 million, but now you can start companies for $10,000 by building an app or a website. You try it, and see what works. This generation is able to do this kind of trial and error, a very measurable process. That's much of what we're doing at First Round. The key to success is to fail cheap. You can fail often, but you have to fail cheap. Now you can fail cheap, for $50,000, then fail again for $50,000, and then strike it rich with the next $50,000. This way, you've spent $150,000 dollars to start three companies, one of which works. Before, you had to spend $5 million on just one. Kids are doing it in college. Birchbox was started in 2010 at the Harvard Business School. The same year, Adaptly came out from students at the University of Pennsylvania; and Chloe + Isabel was partly built that way in 2011. They're building this in their spare time because it's so cheap."

If the cost of doing business has plummeted, so has the average revenue per user. Knowing how to generate a positive bottom line in spite of this is a great challenge for new startups. "Jeff Zucker, who ran NBC and NBC Universal, has this great saying about the Internet that goes: 'analog dollars are digital dimes,'" says Fred Wilson. "You look at the classified advertisement business on paper and compare it with the classified ad business online, it's a factor of 10. Look at companies such as Zynga, a game company we have invested in. The average revenue per user per month is maybe about $2, and the average player plays a game for about three months, so they extract about $6 per user. In the video game industry, it's about $50 per user. There's this order of magnitude of 10. You get 10 times less revenue in the new model. We need to develop business models, technology platforms, and P&L [Profit and Loss] that could support this idea that the Internet is going to produce a lower range of revenues per user. And it's happening. By lowering the amount of revenue that these companies are trying to extract on a per user basis, they massively increase their market opportunities. Zynga is a good example. Almost 100 million people played Zynga's Farmville game at its peak. I don't know what's the most played video game, but it might not have 100 million players. These dramatically lower costs allow you to reach many, many more users. So these Internet businesses can be very, very profitable on a lower revenue base. Craigslist, the website for local classified advertisements, is the classic example of that. It maybe does a couple hundred million dollars in revenue and maybe a hundred and fifty in profits because it doesn't really have any expenses. Compare it with the traditional classified ad business: it might have billions of dollars in revenue from newspapers, but approximately the same profits as Craigslist because it has so many costs such as call centers, printed paper and so on. And a similar shift is going on from the Internet to mobile devices. The big argument is that mobile doesn't monetize as well as the web. Maybe we're going to go from analog dollars to digital dimes to mobile's pennies, but think about how many more people can have a mobile device versus a laptop!"

Silicon Valley is still the realm of major venture capital firms, with funds of a billion dollars and up, such as the Digital Growth Fund created in 2010 by Kleiner Perkins Caufield & Byers to invest in Internet companies at the growth stage, or Andreessen-Horowitz, the firm founded by Marc Andreessen, of Netscape fame, which is investing a $1.5 billion fund raised in 2012.

New York specializes in a different type of VC fund: smaller, from $100 to 200 million, and more willing to risk financing the early stages of a company. These are the funds managed by Union Square Ventures (four for a total of $600 million); First Round Capital (four funds of about $130 million each); Greycroft Partners (two funds for a total of $200 million and now a third one of $175 million); and Founder Collective (two funds of $40 and $70 million).

"Venture capitalists are changing their models," explains Brian Cohen. "A traditional VC firm exists for the expectation of a $1 billion exit. There are at most two or three of those a year. If you take the last 10 years as a guide, there are more and more VC firms, but how many billion-dollar exits have there been? Very few! Mergers & acquisitions make up for 99% of the exits. What's the average value of those transactions? Maybe $100 million? So the VCs have to change their models. Micro-VC and Super Angels, those are the words they use now."

What has not changed is the way to select the startups to invest in; or rather, whom to invest in. Venture capitalists or angel investors indeed look at the idea and business plan, but they pay particular attention to the people behind the company. Howard

Morgan explains well this approach, shared by all the best "talent scouts" of neo-entrepreneurs: "We basically invest in people because ideas always change a little bit from where they started—not as much as Fab did (Fab.com started as a gay social network and now it's an online retailer with over 1 million members)[2], but they always do. If we have good people, 'heat-seeking missiles,' as my partner Josh Kopelman calls them, who start aiming here but then see that the customers are there, and therefore turn and modify their strategy until they find something that works, then we'll have successful projects. Of course, to evaluate entrepreneurs, we do a lot of reference checks. We talk to people who know them, and we talk to them first to see if they're sympathetic and intelligent. That's what we look for first: intelligence and integrity. Are they honest? That's important because they have to be honest not only with us, but also with themselves when sometimes things don't go as planned. They have to have passion for what they're doing. If they don't have passion, they won't be able to sell to investors or to customers. You can hear it in their voices, you can see it in their excitement about what they're talking about. And they must also be sympathetic, because I'm going to work with these people for 10 years, and I want to be with people I like. Life is too short to spend it with people I don't like! Persistence is also important. They have to stick to it when there's adversity."

16

DIY Funding

Will Crowdfunding Make It Easier to Raise Money?

Thanks to the minimal costs required to launch a company, many startups no longer need venture capital money, notes Don Katz: "Entrepreneurs don't need investors who then push them to realize profits with an early sale. At the same time, they don't need to be screened, in order to obtain funding, by young venture capital associates who have just picked up an MBA but don't understand anything about business. Creative startups are able to disintermediate capital."

They can do it by "bootstrapping," the strategy of minimizing expenses using all possible savings, and the aid of friends and family, to succeed without outside investors. Or with new fundraising tools like crowdfunding as proposed by the JOBS Act (Jumpstart Our Business Startups Act), approved by both Democrats and Republicans and signed into law by President Barack Obama on April 5th, 2012.

The goal of the new rules is to make life easier for startups, or "emerging growth companies" (defined as businesses with less than $1 billion in annual revenue) that can then raise money from small "non-accredited" investors (the "crowd") through specialized crowdfunding sites and without having to make an "initial public offering" of securities.

There are restrictions. Companies cannot raise more than $1 million in 12 months. Individuals who earn up to $100,000 per year, or have assets of less than that figure, may not invest more than 5% of their income (or assets) with a maximum of $2,000 per year. Those who earn, or have assets exceeding $100,000, can invest up to 10% with a maximum of $100,000 in a year. In addition, startups have light disclosure requirements, essentially satisfied with a business plan. Moreover, the limit on the number of shareholders, a threshold requiring a company to register securities, was raised from 500 to 2,000 shareholders.

In practice, the JOBS Act extends the Kickstarter model — funding artists and creators of various products without promising any "gain" in return for the money contributed (as explained previously)— to the investment world. With the JOBS Act, even small investors can dream of hitting a homerun by investing in the next Google.

The association of American venture capitalists, the National Venture Capital Association (NVCA), applauded the approval of the JOBS Act as "much needed relief" for the ecosystem of startups "from the cumulative effect of costly regulations that were dissuading companies from entering the public markets."[1]

"Emerging growth companies represent America's best opportunity for long term economic growth and it is critical that they have access to capital at all phases of their lifecycle," says Paul Maeder, general partner at Highland Capital Partners, and chair of the NVCA for 2012. "The JOBS Act will help revitalize an IPO market that has suffered in recent years under the weight of market volatility and one-size-fits-all regulation. The passage of this legislation sends a strong and welcome signal to our most promising companies that the U.S. capital markets system is open for business."

But some New York investors greeted the JOBS Act with a

degree of criticism. "What is happening in the angel world now," says angel investor Alain Bankier, "is that with the JOBS Act and crowdfunding, with big seed investments given away in the blink of an eye by $1.5 billion funds, with hundreds of overnight Facebook millionaires who are all guys between 24 and 34 and want to invest in their buddies' companies, you have a behavior that is conducive to upward valuations. I think the whole crowdfunding thing is kind of dangerous. I think it's throwing a lot of dumb money into the market."

Brian Cohen is also worried and cautious: "I'm against everything that is not well thought-out and could hurt people. And I think that the early phases of this crowdfunding, that have nothing to do with what we know so far, like Kickstarter, could do just that. I think that crowdfunding is an emotional piece of legislation because everybody wants to do what the rich people are doing. By blasting the floodgates, you create potential for fraud. There aren't systems against it in place yet. It's hard to comment on this, because we're just at the beginning of this journey. The SEC [Securities and Exchange Commission] hasn't even weighed in with their rules and regulations, and they're here to protect us. But, here's the important point. If venture capital firms and angels do so poorly at this game, why does someone think that these people who have the desire to participate will do better? They won't. The returns for those people will be infinitesimally small. If you bring too many investors at the early stage, the companies that move on to later stages will have VCs saying: 'that's ridiculous, you have 50 investors!' That's crazy.' The mechanics of it and the legalities of it get very, very challenging. All of that has to be thought through. A lot of legislation still has to be created."

Cohen explains the work he does with the New York Angels to illustrate the risks of crowdfunding: "If we're not in the same context as the companies we want to invest in, we don't really know what they do. We have to study them a little bit, at least a little bit. It's called due diligence or, at the New York Angels, we call it 'discovery' to make it less intimidating. When I talk to some of my friends who are new angel investors and ask them how much due diligence they do, they look at me and say, 'oh no no no, due diligence is something that you old angels do; we do it from the gut.' Knowing what I know about angel investing, it's just as unprotected sex, you don't know what you're getting. You have to connect yourself to the company, know what they do and what the nature of the business is. Crowdfunding doesn't give you that ability. The other part is, you have to be smart and lucky, and that's the reason why I found Pinterest and had an opportunity to invest. That was because I was in the game. I was in the startup community. I was part of the conversation, so that increased my odds. That's why I call it a contact sport. You have to be in contact with the business and the industry, so that you can really sense it. I used to say that I have a nose for news. I think the same way about angel investing: you develop a nose for it; you can smell it. There are many studies that say that there is a positive correlation between the amount of due diligence and the success of companies. Duh, you do more homework, you get better grades." Cohen calls angel investing a "contact sport" also because those who practice it can get hurt and bleed, lose a lot of money due to the high rate of failure of startups and because it takes a long time, even 10 years, before they can sell the shares. Is it therefore wise to expose this level of risk to investors who don't have the time or the tools to do proper due diligence?

Fred Wilson is more optimistic and offers another perspective: "How can the JOBS act change the dynamic? I think that more ways to get capital is going to be better for entrepreneurs. It may be a little bit of a chaotic and confusing world where there are so many options, and people are saying, 'you shouldn't do this, you shouldn't do that...,' but the more ways entrepreneurs can raise money, the better it is for entrepreneurship, company creation, and the New York startup community. I think that's good. For venture capitalists, I don't know. VCs have benefited from the fact that they had some kind of a monopoly on the ability to finance entrepreneurs once they start to need real money. The venture capital industry might have a worse time, but I think it's better for the entrepreneurs."

17
Space, Talent and Other Challenges
What Are Common Issues for NY Entrepreneurs?

"The biggest challenge for a startup is to find space of any sort, whether it is apartments for the founders and employees, or offices. The day after I graduated from Wharton, I was on the 6 a.m. bus from Philadelphia to come to New York and look for office space. I looked at four; three of them were just not suitable. The only space that was in our price range was way out in the middle of nowhere in Brooklyn. No employee is going to commute, then walk for 15 minutes through factories and then go to the office, especially when you are working late." That's how Rohan Deuskar remembers his first steps in New York with his startup, Stylitics.

Yes, New York is expensive and space is scarce, but all of this should not be "a barrier to success," according to David Tisch. "You should be able to figure out how to live here. You should be able to figure out where to work here. It's expensive, but it's expensive in California too— it's not that easy there. It's an overrated problem. You can find cheap places to live in New York. You can find cheap office space. You can hustle your way early on and, when you're real … it's a pain in the ass, sure, but it's your job, just do it! No one wants to baby people in New

York."

For a startup still in its nascent state, with a team formed only by the founders or little more, your best bet are the co-working spaces or incubators, more and more numerous in the city. When the staff grows and there is need for a real office, the issue becomes finding the right balance between location and price.

The area most desired by the "Three Ms," as the real estate brokers call them—new media, old media and social media—it's Midtown South, stretching from 34th Street down to Canal street, and has his heart in the "historical" Silicon Alley, from Madison Square Park to Union Square. Here an office rental costs an average of $49.12 per square foot per year, about $10 more than Downtown ($39.83), according to statistics from the commercial realtor Cushman & Wakefield (C&W) for the third quarter of 2012. "Rents in Midtown South have touched the highest numbers ever, growing 10% in a year, more than all other areas of New York," says Richard Kennedy, C&W's broker. "Technology companies want to be there to stay close to the enormous concentration of talent in Silicon Alley. But many began to consider even Downtown, where not only rents are cheaper and many buildings have been restructured as high-tech spaces, with high ceilings and open spaces, but there is also a special ambience in the neighborhoods, with European-style bars and tables out in the open, like for example on Stone Street, south of the 'Wall Street bull.'"

Outside Manhattan, startups can find even better deals, from Brooklyn to the Bronx and Queens, as mentioned earlier.

For a startup, even more burdensome than paying the rent, is recruiting engineers. According to Chris Dixon, "if you look at the average venture-backed company—I did the math once—they spend about 4% of the capital raised on rent in NYC. If it's somewhere else, it's about 2 or 3%. You spend so much more on people. Obviously, it's going to be expensive for engineers to live here, but considering that they start earning about $100,000 a year, they can afford it. It's going to be about smaller trade-offs, like living in a smaller place. I don't find that an issue. The rent ends up being not that relevant an issue."

Engineers and software developers are a scarce resource anywhere in the United States, but especially in New York that until a few years ago wasn't considered by these professionals to be a desirable destination. "No one that I remember moved to New York from the West Coast to work for DoubleClick in the late '90s," recalls Kevin Ryan. "We had approached some people to bring them here, but they would say 'it's an interesting opportunity, your company is doing well, but I don't want to move my family because if for whatever reason I'm not working at DoubleClick two years from now, where else can I work? I'm stuck.'"

But with the growth of the New York technological ecosystem, the situation is different now. "I have been hiring people for 16-17 years within a mile of right here," says Scott Heiferman at Meetup's headquarters in the East Village. "I interview people regularly who are moving to New York, and in the past if you asked, 'Why are you moving here?' they would tell you that their spouse had to move to New York or their family was in New York and they had to move. The interesting thing is that for the first time ever in the past year or so, they tell you they move here because New York is where you have to be if you want to work on the most interesting Internet tecnologies. That's new and that's exciting. You know what happens in any history, when something becomes a nucleus or capital of something, it attracts the talent. It's a positive cycle, talent attracts more companies and more companies attract more talent, and that was what happened to Silicon Valley and so I think New York City is in a pretty good spot."

Engineers who decided to work in New York historically went to Wall Street, lured by the high profits in the financial sector. But the market has changed with the arrival of Google and other high-tech companies.

"New York is like San Francisco, it's a city people want to go to," says Dixon. "But in the past, tech people wanted to do finance: I had countless discussions with MIT engineers who told me 'I want to go to a hedge fund.' Or they went to California to work in tech because they thought that they wouldn't have a real career here: they felt this wouldn't be the right place. Now, the fact that eBay is here, that Google and Facebook are here, is important. It's a question of scale. It means that companies can now afford to recruit a bunch of people. It also means that engineers feel that they can have a legitimate career here."

"The best thing that has ever happened to the startup community here is that Google, Facebook, Twitter, Microsoft and eBay have all opened engineering offices in New York," confirms Tisch. That sounds backward, but it's true. Those companies have the resources to bring people to New York. They're going to campuses to recruit people from out of town that will eventually make their way into the startup world. It's bringing better-trained engineers to the city scene."

Dennis Crowley saw this first hand: "If you go to Google's building in Chelsea, one of the biggest buildings in the city, it's full of engineers. For a long time, if you wanted to work in the consumer Internet space, there wasn't much here. If you were a computer scientist or technologist, you worked at a bank, or you commuted out of the city to a research lab at AT&T or IBM. There were a couple of startups around, but Google really showed that you can build a really large consumer Internet engineering organization here in New York. Once they did that, we have been able to recruit more engineers. I went through Google, and a third of the people here at Foursquare have graduated from Google. When we were at Google, we used to sit together at a lunch table. Over the last two years, we've recruited just about everyone from our lunch table at Google, and they're now working at Foursquare. It's not just us: there are a lot of companies that have recruited a lot of ex-Google folks. They've really raised the profile of what it means to be a tech company in New York."

The other side of the coin is that engineers' salaries in New York have risen, and at certain levels are now beyond the reach of startups: the average salary of a software specialist is $114,000 a year, 27% higher than the national average, according to Indeed. A Google engineer who works in New York is paid on average $131,000 (including bonuses and other benefits), up to a maximum of $250,000.

"It's extremely hard to find good employees that we can afford," says Deuskar. In the last year, we've found some developers by going to technology events and we had to convince them that Stylitics was the coolest thing ever, because we couldn't afford to pay them at full price. We have also managed to hire a programmer in Iraq through a cousin of mine. Sometimes we also work with recruiters. Moreover, I've sent personal notes to hundreds of people: we've met the head of recruiting at Gilt Groupe, and the one at Bloomberg L.P. just to try to get friendly recommendations. Part of the problem is that we use Ruby on Rails, programming language become popular less than 10 years ago, and every company, including Bloomberg L.P and American Express, uses that . From a scalability standpoint, it's the language of choice. So the big companies in New York hire every Rails expert, and as a result, we have people with two or three years of programming experience who ask for a $120,000 salary—way out of our price range. But we got better at hiring and at making engineers understand that our startup is a good place to work at. They want to be with other engineers and work on a good technical product, so that their friends will say, 'wow, you're working at Stylitics, that's really cool!'"

Concentrating on the quality of the work opportunity is the right approach, according to Tisch: "Of course hiring engineers is the biggest challenge for any technology growth industry, but that's a long-term problem and an education problem, so it won't immediately fix itself. The better the companies are, the easier time they have hiring. If you ask Foursquare and Tumblr today, it has never been easier for them to recruit because they're real."

The alternative is working with teams of engineers in cheaper countries, a solution adopted by companies such as Fab.com, an e-commerce company specializing in design. "It's been an amazing success, with close to six million members in one year since its launch in June 2011," says Howard Morgan, who has invested in Fab.com. "They've really used the New York design aesthetic. There are many design people here in New York who understand retailing and supply-chain. At the same time, the technology in Fab is all based in Pune, India. Today, engineers are behind a computer, and you don't really know where they are or care about where they are. At First Round Capital we have different companies with really big engineering teams in Romania, Bulgaria, Hungary, St Petersburg, Buenos Aires and all over India. The work gets done. Usually we do the user interface here in the US, so that the English shows up in English and so on. But if you want to move into Europe, we have a team in Germany for Fab.de; if we move to Italy and Spain we'll have teams there too."

Even Zemanta uses this approach, though it's not always easy to handle. "We kept our engineers in Slovenia, because moving the whole team to the US sounded too expensive," explains its founder and CEO Boštjan Špetič. Engineers in Slovenia earn 50% less than their colleagues here in the US, and they are much more stable because there are no Google or Foursquare they can run to. It made business sense to keep the engineering office in Slovenia, and it was evident that we had to have a sales and marketing division in New York. In the end, I fired the people who couldn't work under these conditions, and I paid special attention to hire the right mix of people. And I've forced a lot of communication down between the teams."

The shortage of engineers in New York is a problem likely to remain open forever, according to Ryan: "Look, there's never enough talent. When you hear there's a shortage of tech talent in New York, it's true, and it's due to the success of the city. If you pick any city and, over the next ten years, I tell you there's going to be ten times more openings for jobs in whatever the industry is, you're bound to have a shortage. The growth has been so important that there's no way New York can supply all the engineers you need."

Dixon looks beyond the current boom and is worried about other structural weaknesses in New York: "A lot of people talk about a 'tech bubble,' and I don't think is true. It's reasonable, though, to assume that there will be a downward cycle. If that happens, can New York keep the scale and the momentum going? Or will it be like 2001, when people said 'that tech thing was interesting, but let's go back to the real world,' whereas they kept on building in California? Right now, one real problem is the Internet: we have very bad broadband access in my office. We've tried everything, but I probably have better Internet access at home — it's ridiculous! Plus, it's a building with a couple of other startups, so it doesn't make a lot of sense. The problem is the last hundred feet. There's fiber outside the building, but to get into the building costs a hundred grand, and startups don't want to pay that."

But even bad Internet access can be turned into a business opportunity, according to Tristan Louis: "New York is not always an easy place to live in. Poor bandwidth, inadequate mobile networks and massive population breed adversity. New Yorkers have learned to deal with it and leverage it to create new experiences. Whereas Silicon Valley looks at a way to steamroll a constraint, New Yorkers look at a way to mine it, finding innovative workarounds. So while many look at insufficient bandwidth as an issue, it's led New Yorker to create solutions that can work in the US as well as overseas, in markets where bandwidth is more constrained. I was recently chatting with a New York-based founder who told me that he was relocating his technical team from Ukraine to Estonia because, beyond the cost of employees, Estonian users tend to use slower computers and have less bandwidth. I was confused as to why that would be a good thing so he explained to me that since his company was developing software for mobile devices, it was better to have programmers who knew how to wring every single bit of performance out of a five to ten year old computer because that's the kind of processor you get on a mobile device today. Estonian programmers have been doing that for a long time and it has now become a valuable skill, one he couldn't find in the US markets. I, not unlike many people in both the valley and New York, have often called for more bandwidth as something that is essential to future growth but that entrepreneur showed to me that such a call may not be necessary: smarter use of limited resources may be a more efficient approach and only when we have wrung out every little bit we could, out of the bandwidth and processing power we have, should we start begging for more."

18

A Virtuous Cycle

How Is Academia Interacting with Startups?

"Another difference between New York and Silicon Valley is that Stanford University has existed as a center of the Valley in a way that New York academic institutions never have," Fred Wilson notes. "That has started to change a bit, but academic institutions have been divorced almost entirely from the startup sector that has grown up here in the last 15 years. They're starting to realize that they have to be part of it."

It is not by chance that the Ivy League University in New York, Columbia, is on the hills of Morningside Heights. In the book *The Great American University* by Jonathan Cole,[1] a former provost of Columbia, there are a couple of paragraphs about the role of Jacques Barzun when he was provost at Columbia at the same time that Fred Terman, the "father of Silicon Valley," was provost of Stanford, from the mid '50s to the mid '60s. It is clear that Barzun's idea of the University was a place removed from the world, at the same time that Terman was just getting industrial hooks deep into Stanford.

The role of academic institutions is fundamental to the development of an innovative entrepreneurial ecosystem, according to Chris Wiggins, professor of Applied Mathematics at Columbia and co-founder of hackNY.org: "I spent a lot of time reading about the history of the Engineering school at Stanford and its relationship with startups. I am a firm believer that if you want to build a long-term sustainable entrepreneurial ecosystem you need a critical number of smart people, capital and patience. Academics are useful for two of those ingredients, because academics tend to work on a two-decade time scale. When Terman was the dean of the School of Engineering at Stanford and encouraged Bill Hewlett and David Packard to start Hewlett-Packard in 1939, I contend that he knew that there would be benefits to Stanford in one or two decades, not in one quarter."

"In Silicon Valley, Stanford plays also a big role in stabilizing the economic cycle, constantly going up and down," adds the other co-founder of hackNY[2], Evan Korth, professor of Computer Science at New York University. "Something we did wrong the first time around, in the '90s, was not having a strong connective tissue between the startup community and the academic institutions. We don't have Stanford here, but we have a bunch of really strong universities that, combined, are much bigger than Stanford, and I don't just mean NYU and Columbia, I mean CUNY, Parsons, Pace, and Cornell, and then looking to a bigger circle I think of Syracuse, Carnegie Mellon, and all of these other schools. We must pull them all together and strengthen their connection to the startup community."

A breakthrough in this direction was the decision of Mayor Bloomberg to launch three new projects in the field of applied sciences. Besides the great Cornell NYC Tech campus, discussed earlier, there's the Center for Urban Science and Progress in Brooklyn, created by a consortium led by NYU, whereas on the Morningside Heights and Washington Heights Campuses, Columbia is building the new Institute for Data Sciences focusing on five key areas for the metropolis: new media, financial analytics, cyber-security, health analytics and "smart cities."

In all three cases the role of the municipal administration was to launch the idea via a "competition," rewarding the winning proposal by granting limited space and/or public funds, in exchange for the universities agreeing to invest a lot more money within strict guidelines. Will this top-down effort succeed in replicating the success of the binomial Stanford-Silicon Valley that, according to Wiggins, started instead from the bottom?

"Cornell NYC Tech is literally taken from the pages of Fred Terman and Stanford," explains Wiggins. "After Terman made Stanford 'Stanford,' he was hired by a number of cities to write proposals on how to turn their regions into a Silicon Valley. Among others, Bell Labs and Princeton asked him how to build a new university in New Jersey that was going to emulate Silicon Valley. In his proposal, Terman recommended that they make it graduate only, engineering only, without any emphasis on departments, but with loose focus areas, and an emphasis on training in the local industries. That was in the '60s. Princeton and Bell Labs dropped the plan because of money issues. Today the mayor of NYC is doing exactly what Terman recommended. Is it good for NYC? We won't know for another 15 years. What Bloomberg has done for sure in favor of the NYC tech community is to legitimate startups and change the narrative."

"The one place where Terman was able to emulate his vision again was in Korea with the Korean Advanced Institute of Science and Technology (KAIST)," continues Wiggins. "So there are historical precedents for it failing and there is a historical precedent for it succeeding. But it is something that takes a long time. And the way Silicon Valley happened was a grassroots program, not seeded with a lot of capital by some powerful person, but just people in the trenches creating a project." The implication is that here in New York it is not completely grassroots, but a combination of top-down (the help of the city) and bottom-up (the entrepreneurs, investors and other entities that have been collaborating for years, one step at the time). It is a process that will take a long time before reaching the levels of Silicon Valley.

A true bottom-up program is hackNY, founded on February 23, 2010 by Wiggins, Korth and Hilary Mason. Every summer it offers a group of computer science students the opportunity to work, for pay, in New York startups. The students are mentored, are involved in real projects, and interact with the best brains in the NY technological community. Trainees were 12 the first year, 35 the second, and 31 in 2012—relatively few because managing the program is time-consuming, and Wiggins and Korth are doing this as an extra on top of their daily responsibilities as University faculty.

In addition, hackNY regularly organizes "hackathons," 24 hour marathons where New York startups present their products and students build original applications for them. These competitions of digital creativity are becoming very popular, with hundreds of students from all over the northeast and Canada. The winners of the HackNY hackathons are then recognized at the New York Tech Meetup.

There is even a startup, Hacker League, created by three students to help those who want to organize new Hackathons. "Two of them are hackNY fellows," says Wiggins. "In fact many of the hackNY fellows have started their own companies and raised money from investors, others have gone to work with some of the best startups or with VC groups. Two of our hackNY alumni are becoming venture capitalists themselves. One is working as an analyst at Union Square Ventures. So the students have gone on to hire one another."

"Feeding this virtuous circle between the academic environment and the adrenaline of a startup is precisely the aim of hackNY," adds Wiggins: "We founded it as a way to catalyze the relationships between smart people and capital, both now abundant in New York. We believe it's a program that will benefit NYU and Columbia, and New York City more generally in one-two decades as opposed to one-two quarters."

The two founders of hackNY were tired of seeing their students sucked in by Wall Street or moving to California. "Silicon Valley's origin was in the Stanford engineering faculty in the '30s and '40s. They wanted the talented students not to leave Silicon Valley and go to the East Coast, the incumbent at the time," says Wiggins. "Now we are in New York, a place where we have two incumbents. We have a local incumbent, Wall Street, taking away many of our students, and we have a West Coast incumbent in the form of Silicon Valley. New York technologists and engineers who want to foster innovation have to fight against these incumbents. That was very much my thinking for the last decade, because I have watched these really smart people either go to positions in financial services that they hated, or make the assumption that if they wanted to do something interesting and technological, they had to go to the West Coast."

"I have had many students who went into financial services and hated the experience," Wiggins continues. "They work long hours on something they don't believe in, and their individual contributions don't have an eventual effect on shaping products or economies. They work hard at things that they find meaningless. They wish they had a more informed and active decision-making process about their own future rather than simply doing the things that seemed the most obvious and that were artfully and skillfully sold to them by recruiters in the financial services industry."

Wiggins and Korth found themselves talking about this right after Lehman's 2008 collapse, and hackNY's idea took shape in 2009 in order to seize the moment of the loss of luster by

Goldman Sachs and the other big banks on Wall Street. "We felt we needed to build something immediately, before the banks came back with their large volume hiring, but also before the narrative for the young people returned to 'the obvious thing to do is financial services.' We wanted to create some sort of counter-narrative," recalls Wiggins. "We talked about this in 2009, feeling there was a need for some stable, focused and mission-driven attack on ignorance, because the thing that's keeping engineers from going into startups, I believe, is just ignorance of the fact that there is this startup community that desperately wants to hire them, that will offer them technically interesting problems, and autonomy of what they work on."

Each year, the applications for entering the hackNY summer program grow, and on New York campuses today, startups are the new fashion. The confirmation comes from the flourishing of clubs devoted to high-tech entrepreneurs. Mark Peter Davis created one of the first ones in 2006 at Columbia, while he was still attending Business School. "There was nothing that connected all the people interested in startups at the University level, without distinction among the various schools, so I founded the Columbia Venture Community (CVC) to organize debates among experts, demos from new companies, networking events. Then a friend of mine did the same at NYU and in the same spirit we created the New York Venture Community." Mark then went on to become a co-founder of Kohort and a venture partner at High Peaks Venture Partners.

The student mentality is unlike the '90s: "the typical student we have at hackNY is not doing it for the money," says Korth. "That's what we are looking for, the student who wants to change the world. I think it's a narrative that did not exist five years ago and, for good or for bad, Mark Zuckerberg played a large role in creating it. It was different in the '90s, when there were no organic student groups forming startups on campus. I'd like to think that I helped catalyze some of it, but it's a national story. When I was in high school the first *Wall Street* movie came out and a lot of my classmates ended up on Wall Street trying to become kings of the world. *The Social Network* was the equivalent for this generation."

The title that New York University conferred on Korth a couple of years ago, is symptomatic of the change of sensitivity in city academic institutions. In addition to Clinical Associate Professor, he is the "Faculty Liaison for Technology Entrepreneurship." It is a special recognition of the role of a professor with a very special background. In fact, Korth got tenure in 2003 without having obtained a doctorate, but with an M.S. earned while working at a startup, and also after other experiences in business and science. An amateur programmer since he was 11 years old, Korth did not study computer science in college, because he got "distracted," as he likes to say. His first job was as a sports agent for female basketball players. Then, in the mid-90 's, he decided to study for a Master's degree in Computer Science at the Courant Institute of Mathematical Sciences at NYU. In '99, two events marked his career. In order to overcome his fear of public speaking, he asked (and got) to teach a course at NYU. Not only did he improve his public speaking skills, but in the process he discovered his love of teaching. At the same time he went to work for a startup, AfterNIC, in order to fulfill a course requirement: an information technology project.

This course took groups of students and paired them with companies to build software for each company. "The year I took it, the companies I had to choose from were a bunch of big companies, mostly financial, and then this startup called AfterNIC," remembers Korth. "I ranked that one startup as my first choice and the professor gave it to me. At the end I was the only person in my class who was hired by that company. It shows how many barriers I had to overcome to get hired by a startup using university resources." Working full-time at AfterNIC from January 2000, and having received his Master's in May of the same year, Korth also became shareholder of the company that, two months later, in the summer of 2000, was sold to Register.com for $48.6 million—one of the last large acquisitions of the period. With the money he made, Korth traveled the world, returned to New York, did some consulting, and started to teach at NYU, eventually getting his tenure, but without ever losing his passion for startups.

"In 2003, along with some friends from AfterNIC, I was the founding chief scientist of a company called NowPublic, where we pioneered the citizen journalism space," says Korth. "It was sold in 2009 to Examiner.com. So during this entire period, I became the guy who hangs out with students at NYU. I coached our programming team, and in 2004 we won the greater NY region competition. I am also the academic advisor of the ACM (Association for Computing Machinery) and two years ago I helped students found Tech@NYU, practically the NYU tech entrepreneurship club. That's what I love about my job: being around young smart people who want to change the world, and encouraging them to be crazy enough to try to change the world."[3]

New York is not only trying to replicate the Stanford-Silicon Valley development model. It also wants to be a leader in promoting the study of sciences, including engineering, computer science, and software design at all levels of schools before college. In September 2012 the Academy for Software Engineering high school opened in Manhattan, and in Brooklyn the Pathways in Technology Early College High School started its second year—two pilot projects of the local public school system that, if successful, could expand with the support of technology companies.

"I think you have to push tech education as far down the

education stack as possible, and I literally mean kindergarten," says Korth, who is involved in several of these projects and is also doing research on computer science education for children and teenagers. "If you expose little kids to this stuff, they are more likely to know it's an option. I'll never forget my friend's kid looking at the LCD on a digital camera and trying to enlarge it by pinching the screen—and he's two years old. He was doing what you do with an iPhone but the camera does not have that functionality, and he was like: 'What is this? It doesn't work!' I think to solve the diversity problem of computer scientists, to solve the demand for people who know how to write code, to solve the gender issue, the key is to push technology all the way down, so that the students who are naturally inclined in that area find that it is an option. If they are not exposed until college, it's too late."

The road is long, stresses Korth, citing the bipartisan law "No child left behind," approved in 2001 to improve the American pre-college education system. In a thousand pages of text, Computer Science is never mentioned as a subject to be considered.

Among the many private initiatives in this field, the latest, launched in the summer of 2012, is aimed at middle-school female students in New York. Girls who Code is a seminar, hosted by a startup (AppNexus in 2012), where 13-17 year-old girls learn how to write software programs, design websites, and build applications. Mainly, they learn that these subjects are fun and accessible to them, and not only to male computer geeks. "Girls who Code is not just a program, it's a movement to close the sexist gap in the technological sector," explained the program's two organizers, Reshma Saujani and Kristen Titus, to attendees of a big gala that took place on the evening of Oct. 22, 2012 on the floor of the New York Stock Exchange. The occasion was to celebrate the success of the first edition of Girls Who Code and collect additional funds in support of the initiative. The first 20 "graduates" of the course spoke of their experience and their dreams for the future, while sitting at the gigantic table in the NYSE's Board Room. Tomorrow, one of them could return as the CEO of a high-tech business, and perhaps ring the bell on the trading floor to inaugurate her company's Initial Public Offering.

19

Beyond Consumer Web

Are There Other Promising Technologies in NY?

"In the first 10, 15 years of the Internet, New York became very strong or even dominant in the consumer-facing Internet companies' world. But in enterprise software, San Francisco is still the dominant place for now. Nevertheless, you're starting to see the 10gens of the world come up," notes Kevin Ryan, co-founder of 10gen, often cited as an example for a new generation of startups emerging in New York.

The product 10gen is famous for, MongoDB, is an open source document-oriented database system whose genesis is linked to the New York advertising world. In fact it was developed starting in 2007 by the co-founder and former chief technology officer of DoubleClick, Dwight Merriman, with one of DoubleClick's R&D engineers, Eliot Horowitz.

Fred Wilson recalls the birth of MongoDB: "It came out of the scalability problems that DoubleClick had. They were serving 70-80% percent of the display ads on the Internet and, as the Internet kept growing, they had to serve more and more display ads and constantly ran into problems, taking the technology of that time and getting it to operate at the scale they needed it. So they believed that someone had to create an

Internet scale database from the ground up. The founders of MongoDB just happened to live here in New York, they got this experience working for DoubleClick and said, 'This is a problem that has to get solved,' and they went on to solve it in New York. That's a company that you more likely would see in Silicon Valley, but the fact that they were successful in creating that company here suggests that you can build that kind of company in New York, and there probably will be more of these kinds of companies here. But it's still not the thing that New York is known for, and it won't probably be for quite a while."

Ryan is more confident: "The perception is still that for hardcore technologies you need to be in San Francisco, but that perception is going to change in the next few years. The talent is here, and 10gen is the first example of such a company. Six years from now, I bet there will be three other companies in New York, probably from people who worked at 10gen at some point, young engineers who broke off and started their own thing that will add to the growth in that area. San Francisco is in its seventh generation of entrepreneurs, while New York is in its second or third, so of course we're much smaller than San Francisco in enterprise software. It really boils down to talent."

Even Alan Patricof thinks that New York is on the right path: "Pure technology companies are still based in Silicon Valley. But with the new Cornell campus and the focus of the city on enterprise software, I think we're going to see a change in that over the next several years. I'm optimistic. This is going to be a more technology-oriented environment, important in attracting more engineers and software designers, and even in making software companies move here."

This trend has already begun, and an example cited by Patricof is Infor, the world's third largest supplier of enterprise applications and services, that in the spring of 2012 decided to move its headquarters to New York from the suburbs of

Atlanta, Georgia. Founded in 2002, Infor is a large company with over 12,000 employees, offices in 40 countries, 70,000 customers worldwide and revenue of nearly $3 billion. Their offices in New York, near the Flatiron district, employ 75 people that should grow to 200 by 2014. CEO Charles Phillips, former President of Oracle and managing director of Morgan Stanley, created in New York a "Design Division," initially comprising a dozen engineers and designers tasked with modernizing its products. It is true that Silicon Valley has more engineers, but those rooted in the New York startup culture "are younger, more aggressive, and willing to take more risks," said Phillips to Crain's New York Business, explaining the choice of moving to Manhattan. Other factors he cited were the proximity to Europe, where Infor has 40% of its business, and expectations around new Cornell-Technion applied sciences campus on Roosevelt Island, where Phillips hopes to recruit young talent.

"If the Cornell-Technion campus works out right, we'll see a little more hard technology," confirms Howard Morgan, emphasizing Wall Street's role in pushing for a diversification of the types of startups in the city. "New York will always be a great user of hard technologies for the financial sector. We have invested in a company, MemSQL that commercializes the world's fastest database. They're based in California, but in June 2012, to launch their product, they came here, where the financial industry is. In fact MemSQL can do a million and a half ticks per second on their database, or about 30 times faster than most existing databases. Who needs that? Well, Bloomberg processes 45 billion ticks a day, and the high speed trading guys want to process large quantity of feed traffic as well. Where does MemSQL come from? Facebook, which processes half a million 'likes' per second. The need for this database started at Facebook, but the high paying customers will be here in New York and that means hiring a salesman here and working with the New York community to understand the particular application details and needs."

Beyond enterprise software and database systems, the technology sector in New York can also develop in other directions. That's what Micah Kotch hopes: "I would like to see the city embrace things such as health care IT or energy IT, what we call 'clean web,' and really expand and look to get smart people working on problems that really need to be solved. New York City should not try to replicate Silicon Valley. We're not Silicon Valley, and we'll never be like Silicon Valley. But if you look at California's track record for deal flow and volume, they have really a sophisticated network in health care and life sciences, and that kind of sector diversity is something that New York really needs to encourage."

In order to encourage the emergence of startups in the field of health, several incubators and accelerators were created in New York by 2011: StartUp Health, Health Blueprint, WellTech, Health 2.0 and the New York Digital Health Accelerator, the latter with the support of the Department of health of New York State and of the Partnership for New York City Fund.

"We are trying to stay a step ahead of the established industries," explains Maria Gotsch, President and CEO of the Partnership for New York City Fund. "Right now we are not focusing on IT or Internet startups anymore, but rather on programs that can help seed new industries. Hence the New York Digital Health accelerator, the BioAccelerate Prize and New York Tech Connect, which organizes events that bring together scientists and engineers who want to build products and create new technology. We are also thinking about Big Data and genomics research." The Partnership for New York City Fund was established in 1996 as a private partnership, not a government fund, with the support of "the city's financial and business leaders to help build a stronger and more diversified local economy," says Gotsch. Another industry we believe in is fin-tech [financial technology], because it's rooted in one of the real strengths of New York. That's why we established the Fintech Innovation Lab, a unique accelerator program where each fintech company is paired with two industry people from New York financial institutions, who can give the company a good sense of how competitive and needed its products are."

But it is mostly from the creation of the Cornell-Technion campus, NYU's Center for Urban Science and Progress, the Institute for Data Sciences and Engineering at Columbia, and other new schools and programs in New York City, that we can expect a push into other industry sectors.

20
The Discreet Charm of New York
What Are the Challenges for Foreign Entrepreneurs?

Of all small businesses in New York, 48% are owned by people born outside the United States, according to a study by the Fiscal Policy Institute. Even in the technology startup world, many founders are not American citizens. Sometimes it is a matter of a "brain drain" from countries where it is harder to get financing for an innovative idea. In other instances, foreign-born entrepreneurs use New York as a base to strengthen a business that continues to operate in their homeland. This latter model is often adopted by the Israelis, and now increasingly by the Europeans as well.

For those coming from Europe, the Big Apple has a particular charm. "New York is a pretty popular place for European entrepreneurs, for whom Silicon Valley is too far away," says Fred Wilson. "In the last three months, I've probably met seven or eight teams that are relocating from Belgium, Germany, Scandinavia and Eastern Europe. They're choosing to come here because there's something about the city life that feels more like what they're used to. California is California... Many of these people are taking two or three desks in a co-working space so that they can get grounded, get their bearings straight, and figure out where to go and what to do."

The biggest problem they encounter is getting a visa to work in the US. The United States doesn't offer visas to entrepreneurs, unlike other countries such as Great Britain, Singapore and Chile. Rules on immigration are set at the federal level, and in order to amend them Bloomberg has co-founded the nonprofit organization "Partnership for a New American Economy." From 1995 to 2005, the immigrants helped found a quarter of all American high-tech companies, creating 450,000 jobs, according to the latest available statistics mentioned by Jeremy Robbins, Special Advisor on these issues for the Office of the Mayor of New York City, and Director of the Partnership for a New American Economy. Bloomberg has often stressed that immigrants are a major driving force in the economy of New York, yet they often struggle to get permission to stay legally in the United States. H1B Visas are reserved for highly specialized personnel, and are very few compared to the needs of the high-tech sector. In addition, they are often denied to the founders of a startup, who may have a more managerial role without meeting specific professional abilities required by law. The EB-5 program, on the other hand, offers a green card to anyone who invests at least $500,000 creating jobs, but has only been used so far for real estate projects such as the new Barclays Arena in Brooklyn.

Bipartisan reform proposals recently have been presented in Congress: the Startup Act 2.0 wants to establish a new type of visa for those with $100,000 of capital and employing at least two US citizens in the first year of US operations, and five over the following three years. After four years, the owner is eligible for a green card. But the political process won't be a stroll.

The sort of candidate who might have benefited from such legislation is Boštjan Špetič, a Slovenian citizen, discussed previously. As founder of Zemanta, Špetič had opened his business in New York in 2009 with an L-1A visa, used to transfer a foreign company's top managers. Zemanta had an office in London and Špetič had moved to the USA from there. After a year, however, he was denied a visa renewal. "The US officers said that we didn't have enough staff in the United States to justify a senior executive position," recalls Špetič. "They stated that it was obvious from the organizational chart that we didn't have an office manager, implying that no one was answering phone calls, and that's why we could not claim a senior executive transfer. Somewhere in my office I still have four pages of explanations. At that point, I called everybody, the American ambassador in Slovenia, the Slovenian ambassador here, the Slovenian foreign ministry. My investor, Fred Wilson, got in touch with a New York senator, but no one could do anything." Špetič therefore had to work from Ljubljana for the following three months, when a new attorney finally found the right bureaucratic avenue to obtain an L-1B visa, a specialized technology visa.

"Personally, I want to move back home eventually," says Špetič. "I'm not looking to permanently immigrate to the US. I prefer the European lifestyle. Nevertheless, this is absolutely the best place to build a startup, especially in the media space. It made so much sense to build and grow the company here. I never could have done it in Europe, and that is an amazing achievement for New York City."

For this reason, when other European entrepreneurs ask him for advice, Špetič always tells them to settle in New York, at least for a period of time, to gain American experience. And for them he dreams of creating a co-working space modeled after WeWork Labs: "Imagine a place exactly like this, but with decent coffee, wine tasting events in the evening and only non-US business people working in its offices," explains Špetič. "There is a set of problems that foreigners have that Americans just can't understand. Visa issues are the most obvious ones.

Working-with-remote-teams issues, travel issues, personal issues such as which schools to send your children to... It's a set of things that is different from what American startups talk about. You don't need networking events for foreigners because you want people to network into the New York community, but a working environment would make sense because it would be like a safe haven, an extra comfort zone for foreigners with a different work culture."

The dream of Elio Narciso—Internet entrepreneur and angel investor who, since 2004, shuttles between Italy and the United States after having earned an MBA from the MIT Sloan School of management—is to open the New York location of the Talent Garden (TAG) network of co-working spaces. One of his latest creations, Yoodeal, operates between New York and Milan. Yoodeal is an online personal shopping service created in March 2011 and currently launched in Italy and Spain, but soon to be launched in other markets. New York boasts another startup founded by Narciso in 2009, mobAVE, that does business in the field of mobile advertising. "From New York, I often use resident European talent for my startups," says Narciso, who in 2012 became a TAG partner. Talent Garden already has a presence in Bergamo, Padua, and Turin, in addition to Brescia, where the company was founded at the end of 2011.

"Our dream is to launch a TAG ecosystem in every city in the world, an idea based on the Silicon Valley example," you can read on their website. "We hope to build a big community of minds, a vast network of shared resources where every single member has the best possible opportunities to develop ideas and projects, independently of where in the world they may be from. Talented people should be able to collaborate with one another and interface with businesses, entrepreneurs and the media anywhere in the world as well as in their own country."

The same principle of exchange of ideas and collaboration among technological communities in various countries has inspired the decision to bring General Assembly, the "school-incubator-co-working space" mentioned previously, to Europe. At present, GA has locations in London and Berlin, and is considering opening spaces in other cities, "But," warns co-founder Adam Pritzker, "there must first be local demand for these initiatives. The way we go into any given city is by building a community first. We do classes, workshops and events, and once we feel comfortable that there is a big enough community and a big enough need, that's when we start thinking about building more infrastructure."

Founded as a commercial port for Dutch companies, New York remains faithful to its origins as a junction in the circulation of people and businesses between Europe and the United States. It is the basis for a growing number of "bridge" initiatives between the two continents.

One is the Italian Business and Investment Initiative (IB&II), founded by Fernando Napolitano together with its COO, Gianluca Galletto. After a career of almost twenty years in management consulting for Booz & Co., where he was Managing Director of the Italian subsidiary and head of its European Advisory Board between 2002 and 2009, Napolitano decided three years ago to move to New York, embarking on a mission to promote Italian business ideas in the US and attract American capital to fund them. "We offer a complete platform, from financial advice to legal and marketing for businesses and institutions that want to do business in the United States, including looking for investors," says Galletto. Napolitano, who is also on the board of Italian power company Enel, had begun six years ago to encourage Italy-US exchanges via the Fulbright-BEST Scholarship, sponsored by the US Embassy in Rome: "I am Chairman of the Committee that selects the young Italians," says Napolitano. "We brought 53 of them under 35 years of age to study entrepreneurship for two months in the United States and from this project 26 Italian startups were created."

Since last year, Napolitano has also joined forces with Mind the Bridge Foundation, founded in 2007 in San Francisco by former Googler Marco Marinucci, to launch the first American venture capital fund focused on Italian startups. "The Fund started with personal investments of some top managers and entrepreneurs such as Francesco Storace (Enel Green Power), Giovanni Perissinotto (former Generali) and Fedele Confalonieri (Mediaset)" says Napolitano, himself an investor in the Fund. "Now we are collecting signatures of American institutional investors." An example of the initiatives organized by IB&II was the Nov. 28, 2012 Symposium at the conference center of law firm Loeb and Loeb in New York, where 12 Italian consumer and "mobile" startups presented. These companies, financed mostly by Italian investors but looking for other funds and business opportunities in America, included: ADmantX, ArtistFan, Beintoo, Homply, HyperTVx, Blomming, iCoolhunt, Mosaicoon, +Plugg, Real Made In Italy, Stereomood and Timbuktu.

Another reference point for foreign startups that want to explore the opportunities offered by New York, is VentureOutNY, founded in 2012 by the 29-year-old American Brian Frumberg. "Until May 2011 I worked for a financial startup that was purchased by Standard & Poor's," says Frumberg. "Then I decided to get back into the world of startups, and while I was looking for a business idea, I found it at an event at the Canadian Consulate in November 2011. There I discovered that even that country's entrepreneurs, so close to us, have trouble orienting themselves when they come to New York seeking partners, funding and business opportunities. The high-tech community in New York is generous, but very broad. It takes some time to decode it and really get into it. If you are here only with a three-month visa you have to do it quickly."

VentureOutNY wants to help international startups understand what they can do in New York, not only by providing information, but also by organizing events such as that of Oct. 11, 2012 entitled German Innovation Showcase. This was a parade of five German startups, selected with the help of consulting company iFridge, and "judged" by a panel of three experts: Joy Marcus, venture partner at DFJ Gotham Ventures; Yanev Suissa, a Venture Fellow of New Enterprise Associates; and Mark Fasciano, co-founder & managing director of Canrock Ventures. The subsequent event was dedicated to British startups. Long-term, even Frumberg likes the idea of creating in New York a co-working space or an incubator for foreign startups.

How to navigate the US immigration system was the central theme of the first meeting of the NY-Tech-International Meetup, held on Nov. 7, 2012 by Arthur Bierer, software developer with nearly 20-years experience in high-tech and co-founder of AbDevLabs. There were young entrepreneurs and freelancers from all over the world: Australia, Canada, South Korea, Estonia, France, Germany, Great Britain, India, Italy, New Zealand. All were hanging on every word of Michael Petrucelli, founder and Executive Chairman of Clearpath, a startup dedicated to helping those who must apply for work visas in the United States. "There are 93 different categories of visas and it is important to understand that they do not correspond to the reality of business, but follow their own special logic," explained Petrucelli, who was in charge of the new US Citizenship and Immigration Services (USCIS) bureau formed after Sept. 11, 2001 within the Department of Homeland Security (DHS), as well as an official of the Department of State, and thus has an intimate familiarity with the mentality and the language of the federal bureaucracy. His experience was the basis for starting Clearpath, a web service aimed at helping applicants understand the best visa for their needs and apply for it in the proper way.

According to Bruno Cilio—Managing Partner of New York's law firm Cilio & Partners, specialized in assisting Italian entrepreneurs coming to the US—the best avenue is to ask for an E2 visa. "In order to get it you must have capital at risk in the new business," explained Cilio. "Usually it takes $100,000, even if they are borrowed. But the number could be lower, as long as you can demonstrate that the capital is sufficient to operate in the sector you are targeting. That might be the case for an Internet company, for example, where costs are often reduced to the minimum necessary. The company has to be at least 51% owned by the person asking for the visa, and must further commit to hire a number of US citizens commensurate with its plans. For an Internet company it could be just a couple of people." It is a solution, however, only available to those countries, such as Italy, that have signed a trade agreement with the United States.

"But NY-Tech-International Meetup does not just want to facilitate transfers from abroad to New York," says Bierer. "I also spoke to many people who want to go from here to other countries to build startups or find a market for their products. This International Meetup can be a place of exchange in both directions." It is definitely one of the networking opportunities where foreign entrepreneurs seek valuable contacts to realize their dreams.

Davide Rossi, for instance, a 36-years-old Italian mechanical engineer who, after working in the family business (model racing cars) and in the oil industry in Qatar and India, earned an MBA at MIT in 2010 and remained in the United States, stated: "I work with a California-based software company, but I'd rather stay in New York because I find it easier to build a network of contacts here," says Rossi. "I am passionate about the 'Internet of Things' and I'm studying a product in this field. I am looking for a co-founder and I will recruit design engineers based in Italy, because here they are too expensive."

Another Italian hunting for partners and funding in New York City is 35-year-old Alessandro Santo, graduate in economics at Bocconi University in Milan and with a Columbia MBA. "I worked for a prestigious Italian asset managers, Euromobiliare, and then in consulting for Bain, but in my heart I've always been an entrepreneur," says Santo. "That's why in 2008 I left the safe position and excellent salary of Bain and Co. to join dPixel, an Italian seed stage fund created by Gianluca Dettori (founder and former CEO of Vitaminic, the first Italian music distribution business that completed a successful IPO in 2000) and focused on startups. And in September 2012, I launched my own startup together with Pietro Montelatici and Massimo Montagnana: Homply, an innovative service for those seeking a home on the web and on mobile. I would like to incorporate the business in the US because I believe the culture and environment here are the right ones, focused on development and open to a thousand possibilities." (Homply was one of the startups featured at the December 2012 IB&II conference).

The Bloomberg Administration does everything it can to attract talents to New York. The NYCEDC has launched a series of initiatives aimed at international audiences. For example, every year it organizes two competitions: "NextIdea NYC," a competition among global business plans, with a paid trip to New York to meet investors and $35,000 prize; and "NYC Venture Fellows," a program for 20-30 "rising star" entrepreneurs selected from around the world, who are mentored and helped in opening their activity in New York.

All information needed to start a business is on the website of the city, where in particular the section "Business Express" helps aspiring entrepreneurs understand which rules to follow and what incentives are available. "It is the result of Bloomberg's effort to put everything online in a transparent manner," says Carlton Vann, Director of the Division for International Business within New York City's representation at the United Nations: an "ambassador" who works mainly with the Chambers of Commerce and foreign trade institutes of other countries, as well as international organizations such as the IB&II. "We also provide practical information to find legal advice or administrative and office space," says Vann. "We have for example an agreement with the New York State Bar Association, where a foreign company who wants to settle here can have a free one-hour consultation with an attorney and then they are free to choose whomever they wish for legal representation."

Speaking of the United Nations, an original proposals to solve the problem of entrepreneurs who wish to settle in New York but do not have a visa, comes from David Teten, partner of ff Venture Capital and "citizen of the world" (he lived in Israel, France, Brazil, Chile and Taiwan). "An ambitious, although expensive idea would be to set up a 'virtual seastead,' perhaps on U.N. headquarters territory, for high-quality entrepreneurs who do not have US visas," says Teten. "A team in California is already creating an offshore seastead for non-US citizens who want to build companies in the US. The U.N. headquarters in New York is technically located on 'international territory.' Perhaps it is possible to set up an apartment building near the U.N. HQ as a virtual seastead. I spoke with the Seasteading Institute, who is looking into this idea. Or we could simply launch a seastead accelerator offshore from New York." Hurricanes permitting ...

21

If It Looks Like a Bubble …
Are We in for Another Rude Awakening?

The enthusiasm you can feel within the New York technology community raises obvious comparisons with the Internet mania of the '90s. The startup boom and the growing number of people who call themselves "angel investors" beg the question of whether we're creating a new "bubble." Of course it is different today since there is a dearth of IPOs, while at that time they were numerous and billions of dollars of institutional and individual investors' money were wiped out when the bubble burst. But among the few IPOs of the past two years, the one that was most eagerly awaited, Facebook, ended up at the center of a huge controversy around its valuation and the general over-valuation of new Internet companies. New York played a particular role in this story. It was on the "alternative" online marketplace, Second Market, a New York-based company, that Facebook shares had been skyrocketing, to over $40 per share, before the Initial Public Offering on NASDAQ; and it was also taking into account those semi-official quotes that investment banks priced the IPO at $38 per share, well above where Facebook share price would eventually settle.

Some of the protagonists of the high-tech world in the Big

Apple are worried by some indications of new excesses, but the majority firmly rejects the idea of a Bubble 2.0.

"It was pretty bleak in New York until 2007," observes Chris Dixon. "You'd go to a party and say that you were a high-tech entrepreneur, and they would think that you were unemployed or something. Now, you risk going the other way: it's too trendy. There has to be a happy middle. The problem when something is too trendy is that it attracts people that shouldn't be in it. When all the Harvard MBAs want to do something, it's probably a bad sign. There's actually a chart that they showed us at Harvard that said that it's a negative indicator. It's a predictor of a cycle."

It is true, there are many people who jump into this business, but that does not mean that it's a new bubble, claims Brian Cohen: "People talk about bubbles and stuff. The bubble we're familiar with, the Internet Bubble, was a bubble just because, when it burst, it hurt people who couldn't afford to get hurt. That's a bubble. Right now, the only people who are invested in this stuff are rich people. If the bubble burst, it wouldn't change my life, and it wouldn't change the life of my friends either, because these people still have more money, right? You have money from all over the world coming to New York right now. But let's make this clear. More money doesn't mean a bubble. It just means more money. More money invested in bad deals just makes these people lose money. Yes, it does create a problem in the model of what's a good investment; it makes the deals a little pricier. But the professional angel investors are suspicious of these deals and won't invest in them. The bad side is that good money is going away, but there's more money behind it."

"I think the bubble is in the number of startups," says David Tisch. "Four or five years ago, there weren't that many companies, so each company had more talent all the way down. There was a depth of talent. I use basketball here, the NBA, as an example. When there are too many teams, the overall product gets worse. When there are too many companies, the talent gets too spread out such that there is not enough depth of talent in enough places to really do great things. I think that this will fix itself naturally over some time. It's hard when there is so much seed money for that to get fixed right away. When everything gets funded, a lot of it doesn't work. Again, it takes something between 16 months and three years for something to fail, so the feedback loop is not quick enough to say 'OK, there is too much of this, this isn't working.' But it's not an economic bubble—there is not enough money at risk."

The Facebook IPO flop could have the positive effect of deflating the bubble that was in the process of forming, says Fred Wilson: "Every pendulum swings too far, and I think that the speculative energy that got built up around Facebook also splashed into a lot of other situations. Facebook raised money before it went public. There was public trading of Facebook shares that was much higher than what we had after it went public. Zynga raised money at $14 a share before it went public, and now trades at less than $3 (as of Oct. 5, 2012). Groupon's last private round of financing was at a higher price per share than the one it trades at now. You look at all that, and you say people got a little over-excited about these things! The pendulum will swing the other way. I don't think it's the end of the world for anything. It just means that the speculative excesses will come out of the system and it will be a little healthier. As an investor, I always like when things cost less."

Alan Patricof on the other hand minimizes the impact of Facebook's IPO on the other startups: "I haven't seen one slight difference. Everything is in a vacuum. Each company is isolated. Facebook is Facebook. Groupon is Groupon. You have Groupon and Zynga collapsing, while other companies are going through the roof. Each company is judged on its own. It's compared to other comparable companies: if the results are positive, the stock goes up; if they're not, the stock goes down. If they have good quarterly results and their earnings go up, the stock will go up again. Groupon is having its problems because of competition, profitability and other real tangible elements. So if you have solid, growing results and solid metrics, your stock is going to go up."

According to John Borthwick, none of what's happening today is comparable to 15 years ago: "Everybody thinks about the bubble and the Internet boom of last time as a single bubble that grew and grew and then burst. It's not actually what happened. What happened was that there was a bubble around e-commerce. Everybody was like, 'Oh my God! e-commerce is going to change commerce.' It was e-commerce, e-commerce, e-commerce... You had pets.com and all these dot-com companies, and that burst. Then, there was a bubble around local search, followed by a bubble in mobile, and so on. So there were five or six sub-bubbles that supported the mega-bubble, the Internet 1.0 Bubble. People ran to 'local,' the next big thing from 1996 to 1998 when I sold my company to AOL, but by 1998 people moved away from local. There were a bunch of things that were fundamentally unstable about what we were doing. For example, people raised a lot of money, lots and lots of money; they would then take about half the money they raised to buy billboards on Time Square or ads for the Super Bowl or on buses to advertise their thing, so they were plowing half the money they raised back into media. Then, they were running like hell to try an IPO with little sense of what the business was. Today, there aren't IPOs going on that have no business model. I think that people are much more rigorous about their business models now. Facebook's IPO may not have gone well, but Facebook is clearly a business. You can argue just how big a business it is. And anyway, what happened with its

IPO is letting some air out of the inflation."

The most convinced in denying that we are living a "deja-vu" is Kevin Ryan: "Look, it's not a bubble at all. I hear that thrown out once in a while. A bubble is when an entire sector is overvalued by an extreme amount. If it's overvalued by 30%, it's just a normal up and down of the market. A bubble is when you get way beyond that. There was a bubble in 1999 and 2000 because, if you took 20 Internet companies and looked at them two years later, they lost probably 80% percent of their values on average. There's no chance you're going to find that here today. I was on TV in 2011 when people said the LinkedIn valuation proved that there was a bubble. I said, "Really? I think it's a pretty good company. We'll see.' Today its stock is more than double its IPO price, because its growth is incredible, its revenues are incredible. The company's great! AOL was up three times in the last year, while Zillow is way down, and also Groupon is way down. So you're going to see a lot of volatility in these companies, but the sector overall is fine. When my company Gilt Groupe raised money at $1 billion valuation, people thought 'Oh my God, this is crazy!' But we raised money at two and a half times revenues: is that a bubble? For a company that's new and growing, it's ridiculous! When DoubleClick was at $12 billion valuation we had $300 million in revenues: that was a bubble! That's what a bubble is. Still, it doesn't mean that companies today are not too overvalued, maybe by 30%, but that's definitely not a bubble. Look, the fundamentals of the whole sector still look great."

According to Ryan, even Groupon is a good example that there is no bubble: "Its valuation got way ahead of itself. But what's remarkable is that Groupon is four years old, and they'll do $2.5 billion in revenues! They're going to sell $6 billion worth of products on their site, and they're going to make $200 million in profits in 2012. So we can debate what the right valuation is, but that's still extraordinary. It got built up in four years! There's clearly value there. We just have to debate whether it's $3 billion worth or 6 or 10, and I think it's close to $3. You're seeing real fundamentals. You're seeing real revenue growth. Every year, you're seeing another 5 to 10 billion dollars of advertising coming online. You're seeing 20 to 40 billion dollars of e-commerce growth per year. Amazon, every year, adds $15 billion in growth. That's unbelievable: that's bigger than Macy's! Every year they're adding a Macy's, which has 150 stores and has been around for 100 years. There's real value here, and it's happening across the board. But, still, it means that out of every 10 companies that will start, six will go out of business, and one will go up and be overvalued. And that means you'll have to live with a lot of volatility and uncertainty. The one trend that you're seeing in the Internet space more so than in other areas, is about fewer, very big winners. Think of TV: for 40 years you had ABC, CBS and NBC. They were all about the same size, and they all did well. In the Internet, that would never happen: one of them would get much bigger, and the other two might go out of business."

22

"This Time Is Different"

Is the NY Ecosystem Sustainable?

"What's different compared to the first boom is that today in the technology industry in New York there is a much stronger sense of community," claims Evan Korth. "At a conference at NYU some of us who had lived through the first phase of Silicon Alley were wondering what we did wrong. And we agreed on one thing: the first time everyone was in it for themselves, everyone on his own, with the sole objective of getting rich. Today, of course people want to make money but, it seems that everyone is in it for NYC, we all root and work for New York to become a startup capital. We all feel part of the New York tech community. And this mentality starts from the top, from Mayor Bloomberg on down."

David Tisch, who is a member of the Council on Technology and Innovation created by Bloomberg in October 2011, agrees on the long-term impact of this mayor: "The Council is a group of about 10 of us who sit down every quarter and talk about initiatives the government is working on. Having a mayor who understands entrepreneurs is an incredible value. His long-term thinking has been incredible. The Roosevelt Island campus, the technological high school, these are long-term initiatives that will have long-term value. Will they help the hiring needs of current startups? No. Will they have positive effects on this community in the long run? Yes. I think that's awesome. There's a real commitment on the part of the government to invest in technology and entrepreneurship, and that is going to establish the city of the future. It's not a fad; it's a foundation! Everything that is happening now is building a foundation for the next 20, 30, 40 years for technology to really be a core sector in New York's economic landscape."

At the end of Bloomberg's third mandate, is there a risk that with the next mayor the growth of New York's tech community may suffer a backlash? No, according to Fred Wilson: "The interesting thing is that the startup community in New York got started without all of the new initiatives—such as the Cornell-Technion campus and CUSP—and this is now getting layered over it. This is going to be healthy for the sustainability of the startup community. It will bring more talent, it will bring more money, and it will bring more glue between the academic institutions and all the smart people. There are some things that might not be sustainable: city and government come and go, for example. The new mayor might not be as favorably inclined to the technology community, and some of this stuff may not come together in a way that I would like it to come together. But I think that the basic fundamentals of the technology sector in New York—having a critical mass of talented people and capital, and being recognized as a large vibrant tech startup community—are all in place and are not going away."

Kevin Ryan expressed a similar opinion: "I don't think that the New York tech community has been so successful because of the Bloomberg administration. It happened on its own. And I told the man, there's actually not that much you can do. The core reason we are doing well here is we have the talented people and the industry here. We've always had that. There are more Harvard MBAs here than there are in any other city in the world. There's just human talent. If you take a tour of the Gilt Groupe's office, one thing you'll realize is that there's nothing here except for people and computers. That's what all Internet companies are, human talent."

The fact that many startups in New York are in the field of new media and are dependent on advertising is not a weakness, according to Ryan: "Don't forget that there is more than $30 billion worth of online advertising invested each year in the US, so there's an enormous amount of money around. It doesn't mean that all the media properties are profitable yet, but that's because there are so many of them. To draw a parallel, now the newspaper industry is still a profitable industry, even though 20 years ago you would have said that it was incredibly profitable. But the real history of the newspaper industry is that it wasn't a good industry for the first 50 years. When there were seven daily newspapers in New York, it was terrible. Then, it went down to six, then five and then four… When it got to one in most cities, it became a great industry. What we're seeing on the Internet is a proliferation of sites and lots of advertising. But there's so much competition that you're going to see consolidation over time, and people will start to make even more money. Remember that Yahoo! is all advertising supported and has always made tons of money. Google makes tons of money too. What you'll see on the Internet is more concentration, so it'll be harder to be small and make a lot of money. Right now in New York *Business Insider* is growing very successfully, and *The Huffington Post* is doing very well. Someone will note that *Business Insider* is five year old, and it's not profitable yet. But when you launch a new magazine, how long does it take for it to attain profitability? Everyone knows it takes five to seven years."

The same new media companies are also making their first steps toward the new mobile platforms where, according to

Alan Patricof, you have the immediate future of the tech business: "The Internet and mobile businesses are in their infancy. There is a long way to go. We have so many new applications. We have the users. The number of people with mobile devices is increasing exponentially across the world. There are going to be more transactions on mobile, more location-based applications, e-commerce and an increasing demand on new forms of content, particularly video. I think we're at the beginning of a big growth in mobile, for a long time to come. It's not going away."

Even John Borthwick believes that "this time is different": "New York's experience in design, data, and social can give this city a platform to be a technological hub that can really be a meaningful part of the economy and be sustainable. Last time, when I started out in 1994 and bought my first company in New York, the crash was devastating to the community. I say devastating simply because we didn't turn a full cycle. We got about 320 degrees around the cycle, and then the 2000 crash happened. To me, the full cycle is about companies being born, growing up, figuring out how to make money, selling, doing an IPO and people coming out of these companies starting companies again. That builds the entrepreneurial terra firma, the foundational material that will make New York a truly sustainable tech city, and that's our job this time. Last time, I think we were almost around the circle, and then the whole thing blew up, with few exceptions such as DoubleClick. So I'm hoping that we can make it all the way around this time. Look at the big companies today, the Foursquares, Tumblrs of the world. If any of these companies have an exit or IPO and you get opportunities for people to cash out in some way and start new businesses, that's what you want. You want to have people who have the experience to bring a startup from nothing to a business and who then take some piece of their gain, decide to reinvest it and start to make money again. These people also make angel investments themselves, so they plant more seeds."

Despite the bubble bursting, "the arc of innovation that relates to media and computing has not let up," emphasizes Borthwick. "I graduated from Wharton in May, 1994 and started my company right up then. I remember that in October I was just getting the team together, Netscape had just shipped their browser. There was an article about it in *Wired Magazine*, not on the cover, but in the middle of the magazine. It was titled 'The next revolution has begun: the World Wide Web.' [1] I remember reading it over lunch on my own and thinking, 'Oh my God! It's going to be six months to a year before all the media companies in the world figure this out, so I have to run really fast.' That was 1994. I think I was right, but I underestimated how big it would be, and in a way I was also completely wrong. Here we are, almost 20 years later, and most of the companies, including the media companies, have no idea what the hell it is, how to work with it, how to relate to it, how to build this and so on."

Today the survivors of the bubble are all doing something different and are all more aware of what a business cycle means, continues Borthwick: "An interesting guy from Web 1.0 is Nick Denton, who in 2002 founded the online media company and blog network Gawker Media. If you interview him, he will say that online advertising does not mean transforming analog dollars into digital dimes, into digital quarters, back into digital dollars. It may just be digital dimes permanently. So Nick is architecting Gawker for that. He has bootstrapped Gawker and has not taken any venture capital. Nick is building a much more sustainable business. Kevin Ryan and Dwight Merriman have a unique model, a little bit of a portfolio approach. They have launched several businesses such as Gilt Groupe, Business Insider, 10gen, Music Nation, Panther Express, ShopWiki. They've thrown about 10 things against the wall and some of them have done well. I've taken a different portfolio approach. And if you talk to Scott Heiferman, who's our friend, one of our investors in Betaworks, he has a special vision for Meetup. He wants to build a company that's sustainable and will exist for 20, 40, 100 years. He has a much longer-term vision for Meetup than practically every Internet entrepreneur you'll run into."

"New York has become the capital of a certain kind of Internet company," says Heiferman. "There is a broad array of types, but companies like Kickstarter, Skillshare, Etsy, Foursquare, Zocdoc, us and others have this thing in common: they are distinctively urban, distinctively about a DIY (do it yourself) culture. The difference between Etsy and eBay is that Etsy has such a tone, a type and a culture that are typical New York tech. Those kinds of companies are such an important part of the future economy. It's the peer-to-peer economy. How people sell stuff to each other, rent from each other, how people build something together, as opposed to Twitter and Facebook diddling around online. There's definitely a bubble in New York, but there will be a category of the Internet economy that will be sustainable and long lasting with these types of companies that are about connecting people to each other, enabling new kinds of markets and unleashing this peer-to-peer economy that New York is a really big player in right now."

Why hasn't New York created a Facebook, Twitter, eBay or Craigslist yet? "It's because New York and also Los Angeles are in love with controlling things; they are in love with directing things and with being gatekeepers," replies Heiferman. "The essence of the Internet is to bring down walls, to empower people, to enable people to build something, to create things. Whereas Hollywood, the magazine industry, the TV industry, Madison Avenue, and Wall Street are about amassing power and control, they are about being a gatekeeper and deciding who is allowed to be written up in a magazine, or who's allowed to be on TV. Culturally it's screwed up! Yes, out of Bubble 1.0 you had DoubleClick and some media companies, but the Internet is not about the media. Facebook is not a media company, it's a communications company."

Who is then creating the future of New York's foundation economy? According to Heiferman it's companies such as Kickstarter, Etsy and Meetup: "We are really saying 'screw you!' to the traditional New York establishment. The future is empowering people to do things themselves. We have on the wall here at Meetup a big sign: not DIY, but DIO: Do It Ourselves. The main thing here is that we are not just changing or building a nice industry in New York, but we are changing the face and the nature of the New York economy, and that is going to be a hard job, it will take a few decades, and at the end of the day it is about changing the world the way it needs to be changed."

Is this really the direction in which the technology industry in New York must evolve to be sustainable? Or is this an unrealistic and maybe utopian program? It is of course the opinion of only a part of the high-tech community in the Big Apple and, if nothing else, it serves to show how diverse and lively the internal debate is, never satisfied with the status quo.

Conclusions and Advice
By Alessandro Piol

When Maria Teresa and I got together in the spring of 2012 and, almost as a lark, I proposed we write a book about technology—Maria Teresa after all is a well-known Italian journalist with expertise in the American tech scene—my first inclination was to write something about technology trends. Terms such as Big Data and Cloud immediately came to mind. After Maria Teresa convinced me that a book should be, yes, informative but also fun to read, we quickly realized there was a much more compelling story to tell: the rise of New York as a hub for technology startups and entrepreneurship.

We are both de facto New Yorkers. I have been living in and around the city for most of my 35+ years in the US, and Maria Teresa and her husband moved to the city in 2000. We both love New York's energy and cultural diversity, and we have always admired the city's ability to recover and rebuild after a crisis. We saw New York's resilience first hand after the tragedy of September 11th, and more recently after the financial crisis of 2008 that led Mayor Bloomberg to help build the technology industry in New York in order to diversify the City's economy. Presently, we continue to see the efforts of many New Yorkers to rebuild parts of the City after the disaster of Hurricane Sandy.

But what is also remarkable to me, having observed New York since the '70s, is how the city has changed and renovated. When I first moved to New York, the country was still reeling from Watergate, New York was bankrupt, and the New York Post had summed up President Ford's rejection of a proposal for a federal bailout of New York with the famous headline: "FORD TO CITY: DROP DEAD." At that time, Times Square was the land of X-Rated movie theaters and "peep shows"; Alphabet City was a combat zone crawling with drug dealers and junkies; and the Meat Packing District was, well, full of butchers. It was a good time to buy properties in the West Village, now one of the sought after and expensive residential areas of New York, but few people wanted to live there. And there was no point in venturing near a city park at night or "exploring" the South Bronx.

Over the course of the past 20 years, under the Giuliani and Bloomberg administrations, the city has transformed itself: street crime has taken a nosedive, Times Square has become a place for families to see shows. Now safer and cleaner, the city has again become an attractive place to live, as many neighborhoods in New York have revitalized and become trendy. There are plenty of restaurants, entertainment and cultural attractions: the younger generations like NY.

This is important to note because having a clean, safe, and attractive environment is a first step to attract new businesses, entrepreneurs, and young people in general. Having lived in the Big Apple for so long, it was amusing for me to hear from several newly minted New Yorkers how happy they are to live in a "safe, clean city with friendly and helpful neighbors." This is not your stereotypical New York image!

Entrepreneurship is not new to New York. All the major industries in New York today were started by entrepreneurs between the mid-1800s and the mid-1900s: the financial industry, the garment industry and fashion, publishing, advertising, TV and entertainment. While New York has had its share of tech entrepreneurs—Alexander Graham Bell and Tom Watson to name but two—the high-tech industry of today is a direct result of post-war government funding grants to a number of Universities around the country. The two regions that first took advantage of this opportunity and fostered the creation of new technology companies were (1) the area around Stanford University, with the founding of Hewlett-Packard in 1939 and eventually Shockley Semiconductor in 1956 (that spawned "Silicon Valley"); and (2) the area around Boston and MIT, where General Georges Doriot (the first venture capitalist) gave Ken Olsen the funds to start Digital Equipment in 1957. In the Greater New York area, however, the substantive research work of AT&T's Bell Labs and IBM's Watson Labs was mostly for internal corporate consumption, and never resulted in the creation of an entrepreneurial ecosystem.

Technology companies in New York started to acquire a profile in the 1970s and 1980s, with the advent of minicomputers and then the personal computer. These new, cost-effective platforms led to the modernization of the banking system, the deployment of Automated Teller Machines (ATMs), and the computerization of trading, to name just a few examples. These projects gave rise to a number of firms, mostly consulting or service firms, serving Wall Street and the financial industry. The early 1980s is the period when Michael Bloomberg started his own company, now one of the largest providers of financial data in the world.

Then, in the early '90s, personal computers with modems were the new standard; online access to information was becoming commonplace and appreciated by users, thanks to services such as Prodigy, Compuserve and America Online; and cable companies were converting to a new digital infrastructure:

the vision of an interactive online future was becoming real. The missing piece, the "light switch," was the commercialization in 1994 of NCSA's (National Center for Supercomputing Applications) Mosaic browser by the compay that would then become Netscape. A revolutionary user-friendly software application that would allow anyone to navigate pages of hyperlinked content accessible via the Internet: the "World Wide Web." Mosaic was the last piece of a puzzle that had been assembling for over a decade, and would open up a new world of opportunities.

Access to the Internet was the great equalizer and one of the reasons why, all of a sudden, so much could happen in New York (and other parts of the country). Before the Internet, it was both difficult and expensive to create an online service for consumers. You would have to compete with established companies such as Prodigy, America Online or Compuserve, which took many years and substantial investment to build. Otherwise, you might find a way to partner with them. If you were providing services to a business, you could do it by using expensive "private networks," one-to-one communication links between provider and customer. One of the companies I invested in the early '90s, Multex, initially was delivering financial information just that way.

With the advent of the Internet, all of a sudden anyone could "hang out a shingle" on the information superhighway, without having to deploy expensive networks or having to compete with entrenched online players as America Online. That's when entrepreneurs such as Scott Kurnit and Kevin Ryan saw the opportunity and decided to start their own companies, with many other talented entrepreneurs to follow. And existing companies, like Multex, were able to provide cost-effective services and faster deployment to an exponentially greater number of customers.

Today, after 20 years of active entrepreneurial activities, the New York tech ecosystem finally seems to be on steady ground. The usual question is: "What happens when the excitement dries up and things start going badly? Will it all fade away just as it almost did in 2000?" There is a certain comfort level in the fact that we have second-generation entrepreneurs, experienced angels and venture capitalists, an active ecosystem with accelerators, incubators, workspaces, service providers, mentors, educational institutions. It feels different than the year 2000, at the peak of the bubble. Yes, there are probably too many businesses being funded, some with marginal or me-too products—not everyone will make it. But there is also a clear understanding, at least among the best investors, that certain segments of the industry are now mature, and that it is more difficult to create large companies in those sectors. And there is much less "irrational exuberance" this time: having "dot com" at the end of your company's name is neither a requirement nor any longer a recipe for success.

The technology business is cyclical, and relies on new waves of technology and innovation for its progress. Silicon Valley and Boston have gone through several such waves. New York has only gone through two such cycles. The first was the advent of the Internet in the 1990s, leveling the playing field and allowing anyone to offer a service on the web. The second, more recent cycle was spawned by the emergence of "social networks," as well as the ability to develop companies with little capital investment—thanks to open source software, cloud services and "lean startup" methodology. It now continues with the migration to mobile on the consumer side, while "enterprise" applications are now fertile ground for investment, thanks to the adoption of social, mobile, cloud and advanced analytics that make sense of the large amounts of data collected from customers.

New York is well positioned to compete in all these areas, but it won't always be a smooth ride, because in fact it is never a smooth ride. The important thing is to persevere through ups and downs—any successful ecosystem demands long-term investment on the part of all stakeholders, a fact that is often misunderstood or underestimated.

Perhaps no one understands the need for a long-term strategy better than Michael Bloomberg, Mayor of New York and himself an extremely successful tech entrepreneur. Through the work of governmental organizations such as the NYC Economic Development Organization (NYCEDC), or in collaboration with privately-backed organizations, like the Partnership for NYC Fund, the Bloomberg administration has laid the foundation for economic development around technology for decades to come.

New York's way of executing on this should be a lesson for others as well: it was not done by throwing loads of tax-payer money at initiatives controlled and managed by the city, but by seed-funding specific projects with little money or underutilized assets, and allowing private entities to do the rest while government got out of the way. These public-private partnerships will bring billions of dollars of investment and tens of thousands of jobs to New York City over the years. The Cornell-Technion engineering campus is a case in point.

In fact education, especially programming and technical training, is of paramount importance to the development of a technology ecosystem. It is not something you can develop overnight, but you can make progress with a combination of long-term and short term initiatives, from internships for high-school and college students, to programming classes offered at the high school level, to more fundamental projects such as bringing a new technology campus to the city, for instance. The Academy for Software Engineering, for instance, is an innovative idea, augmenting the regular high school curriculum with programming courses. If this works, it could be replicated in some of the City's public schools.

We hope that the voices of the many protagonists of this book make clear to every reader that many related elements are indispensable to a strong, innovative, and enduring tech industry: second generation entrepreneurs and investors; a community willing to work together; a supportive but not intrusive local government; tech and entrepreneurial education; the need to take a long term view; and, last but not least, an urban environment that is attractive to entrepreneurs.

But this book is also meant to be inspirational. We think that the type of information we have shared can also be useful for other cities trying to develop similar tech ecosystems. And if we succeed in providing an ounce of encouragement to an aspiring entrepreneur to pursue his or her dream—ideally in New York—we will have accomplished our goal.

The entrepreneur is what the book is about, after all. The ecosystem helps lower the barriers to starting a company, but it is the entrepreneurial team who will define the company, develop a plan, build a product, sell it, raise money, and grow a business. And while we want to inspire new entrepreneurs, it is also important to point out that being an entrepreneur is not easy and not for everyone. So, for those of you who are thinking about founding a startup, let me offer a few suggestions.

1. Don't do a startup because you think you are going to get rich, or because you think it is glamorous. It usually is not glamorous, and the probability is high that you are not going to make money.

2. An entrepreneur is someone who is willing to risk everything in order to change the world. It may sound

like a cliché, but you must have the belief that your idea will make a difference for many people. You must have the ability to execute it, the strength to ignore the negative feedback that is par for the course, and the passion and commitment to be "all in." It takes a lot of hard work to create something that is radical and revolutionary. When work is powerful and meaningful, there is no distinction between work and personal life. You have to be conscious of that.

3. You'll face many obstacles: rejection from customers and investors, rules you need to abide by. Break the rules (without breaking the law)! Push the envelope! Don't take no for an answer! Be persistent! As Jerry Colonna likes to say, you have to be "pathologically optimistic and delusional" to be an entrepreneur.

4. An entrepreneur has a perpetual sense of urgency, is single minded and driven: after all there is only one variable we can control: our work ethic.

5. Work on solving problems that you have experienced first hand, and you have expertise in. That is the best way to ensure that the problem exists and is real. This is the first thing investors will focus on when looking at your company: what do you know about this problem? By the same token, focus on healing real pain points, not minor bruises. A common mistake is to focus on solving problems that exist, but are not high priority for customers.

6. Assess your market. If you are going to be a fast-growing startup, you had better go after a market that is big enough, or that is going to be big. You may have to start with a niche and expand, or ride a trend or an industry or regulatory disruption. Either way, you have to make an honest assessment of your addressable market.

7. Build the best team you can put together. Hire people who are smarter than you. Hire slow and fire fast. Don't let problems fester. Also, balance your team with experience. Younger people who don't know what they don't know are willing to go through walls to reach an objective, but you also need to have more experienced people who understand the consequences and can help clean up the rubble.

8. Get the product out in the hands of customers, or find a way to get feedback from users as soon as possible, so that you don't spend money trying to build something that does not interest customers. If you have to shift direction, or "pivot" as we like to say, figure it out as quickly as possible. If there is nowhere to pivot, and you are destined to fail, fail fast. (Yes, easier said then done. But your investors will remember that you made the hard decisions and returned the leftover cash to them, as opposed to spending it all and running the business into the ground.)

9. If your product has multiple uses, or can be adapted to multiple markets, pick the most promising one and focus on that. If you are successful you can always go after the other opportunities later. If you are trying to go after too much, you'll do everything badly.

10. When dealing with customers as well as investors, be ready to tell your story. Be sincere, transparent, straightforward. There needs to be mutual trust in the relationship, especially with the most important constituencies: your customers and your investors. It may seem obvious, but too often an element of conflict develops when interests should be aligned.

11. Be open to criticism and suggestions. Seek feedback. It's amazing what you can learn from people who have a different perspective. Things that you were not even

thinking about will become obvious to you. Also, seek a mentor, or multiple mentors, early on: people who have domain expertise or experience around the issues you are facing.

12. Finally, don't rest on your laurels at the first signals of success. The journey is long, and you'll need all the help you can get. Be humble, even when you are successful— you can never afford to become arrogant.

Of course there would be a lot more to discuss on these topics, and others that the book does not treat. There are many experienced investors and entrepreneurs who write articles or blogs about these subjects, such as Steve Blank, Jerry Colonna, Paul Graham, Mark Suster, Fred Wilson.[1] I encourage aspiring entrepreneurs to read them—indeed some of the points above have been inspired by their writings.

As a member of the tech industry, researching this book was a lot of fun for me. It was great to sit down with some old friends like Fred Wilson, Howard Morgan, Scott Kurnit, Brian Cohen, Alain Bankier, David S. Rose and many others: all successful people who have been in the industry a long time and can share great stories and many words of wisdom. But it was also an opportunity to get to know some people I had not yet met. Most important, I had a chance to spend time with some of the younger entrepreneurs, to listen to their experiences, and to learn the reasons why they came to New York. Their perspectives were thought provoking and sometimes surprising.

To me, one of the great revelations of this project was to discover how wonderfully helpful the entrepreneurial community in New York can be. CEOs of major companies are willing to mentor younger entrepreneurs. A number of organizations are helping young CEOs refine their strategies, helping them raise money or just provide mentorship. At the end, the sense of community and belonging is a major motivation to stay in one place and not go elsewhere. Building community is always a challenge that any new ecosystem needs to tackle. But once you get there, it's magic!

Maria Teresa and I are deeply indebted to all the people who generously offered their time by agreeing to be interviewed or who otherwise shared their thoughts. We hope you enjoyed reading their stories and opinions.

Alessandro Piol
February 2013

A Startup Guide
to New York

[To access this guide online, up-to-date and with live links, please go to:
http://tech-and-the-city.com/Guide/ or simply scan the QR code above with
your smartphone or tablet]

According to the quarterly **Money Tree report** compiled by the NVCA
(National Venture Capital Association) and PWC
(PriceWaterhouseCoopers), the New York metro area is consistently among
the largest regions of investment, both in number of companies funded and
dollars invested. In 2011 $2.7B were invested in New York, and for the first
time New York passed New England as the second largest region of
investment after Silicon Valley: http://bit.ly/YtUCXL

According to the **New Tech City report**, published in May 2012 by the
Center for an Urban future New York had a growth of 32% in number of VC
deals from 2007 to 2011, compared to negative growth in all of the other
major centers of startup activity: Silicon Valley, New England and Southern
California. The increase in venture capital investments had a positive effect
on the IT sector job growth, with an increase of 28.7% vs. an increase of 3.6%
in private sector jobs for the 2007-2012 period: http://bit.ly/14kqoWD

The **Made in NY Digital Map**, published by NYC Digital, an entity part of the mayor's office for media and entertainment, gives a good sense of the many startup companies and investment firms that make New York their home: http://mappedinny.com/

NYC Digital also publishes **New York City's Digital Roadmap**, spelling out the objectives set by the mayor to make NY a premier Digital City. In order to do that, the city had embarked on a series of Private/Public partnerships to improve education, broadband access, social engagement and government transparency. http://on.nyc.gov/VYyFwN

One of these partnerships is the comprehensive new (coming soon) StartupNYC website, the ultimate directory to over 5,000 startups, investors and New York City services for entrepreneurs: http://StartupNYC.com

Also, don't forget to check out **CB Insights** for further statistics
http://www.cbinsights.com/

NYCEDC site for NYC initiatives: http://bit.ly/14krPnN
A great way to keep track of news is to subscribe to the NYCEDC blog:
http://bit.ly/XCdjBD

A useful "Who's Who" of the New York community was compiled by Steve Schlafman of Lerer Ventures:
http://slidesha.re/10MTHgX

Reading and Discussion

Many veterans of the New York startup world, from venture capitalists to entrepreneurs, write blogs that have become discussion forums in the community. Reading and participating in them is a way to understand what is going on.

AVC (Fred Wilson)	http://avc.blogs.com/a_vc
Chris Dixon	http://cdixon.org
Continuations (Albert Wenger)	http://continuations.com
Gotham Gal (Joanne Wilson)	http://www.gothamgal.com
Innonate (Nat Westheimer)	http://innonate.com
MPD (Mark Peter Davis)	http://mpd.me/#blog
Reaction Wheel (Jerry Neumann)	http://bit.ly/14fBUn3

Redeye VC (Josh Kopelman)	http://redeye.firstround.com
Strong Opinions (Mark Birch)	http://birch.co
ThisIsGoingToBeBig (O'Donnell)	www.thisisgoingtobebig.com
Way Too Early (Howard Morgan)	http://bit.ly/WY4i7J

NY publications with good coverage of New York news include:

BetaBeat	http://betabeat.com/
Silicon Alley Insider	http://www.businessinsider.com/sai
The New York Times Bits	http://bits.blogs.nytimes.com/

Startup Digest has a curated list of major news, including a New York section: http://startupdigest.com/

Startup Genome lets you search for startups, investors, incubators etc: http://www.startupgenome.com/

We Are NY Tech spotlights every day a member of the NY community: http://wearenytech.com/

Educational Institutions

New York is home to several major Universities. Some of them have prestigious specialized Schools or programs focused on media and technology. Here are some of the ones offering undergraduate and graduate degree programs.

City Tech (CUNY)	www.citytech.cuny.edu/aboutus
Columbia University SEAS	www.engineering.columbia.edu
Columbia Inst. Data Sciences	http://idse.columbia.edu
Cooper Union	http://cooper.edu
Cornell NYC Tech	http://now.cornell.edu/nyctech
Courant Institute (NYU)	www.cims.nyu.edu
FIT Baker School Bus/Tech.	www.fitnyc.edu/4404.asp
New York IT	www.nyit.edu
NYU-Poly	www.poly.edu
Parsons School of Design	www.newschool.edu/parsons
Pratt Institute	www.pratt.edu
Tisch ITP (NYU)	http://itp.nyu.edu/itp

There are also a variety of courses and classes offered on entrepreneurship, technology and programming. General Assembly, for example, is a startup incubator but also a campus that offers classes in technology, business and design, while Coursehorse is a site listing a searchable database of classes offered at any point in time in NYC. And there are other programs that offer training in programming and entrepreneurship, both offline and online, as well as "learning by doing" and internship programs. Here's some of the most significant:

Code Academy	http://www.codecademy.com
Coursehorse	http://coursehorse.com/classes-nyc
E[nstitute]	http://www.enstituteu.com
General Assembly	http://generalassemb.ly/education
hackNY	http://hackny.org/a/
Hacker School	http://www.hackerschool.com
Lean Startup Machine	http://leanstartupmachine.com
Sandbox	www.sandbox-network.com
Skillshare	www.skillshare.com
The Flatiron School	http://flatironschool.com

Finally, there are also programs aimed at high school students. The Academy for Software Engineering (AFSE) has just been launched in New York, offering a high school degree augmented by programming courses. And Girls who Code is an organization aiming to prepare 13-17 year-old girls for opportunities in technology and engineering
Academy for Software Engineering: http://www.afsenyc.org/
Girls who Code: http://www.girlswhocode.com/

Competitions

Many of the schools in New York offer business plan competitions. To get up-to-date information it is best to go to a site like BPC that tracks the many events and competitions taking place in New York.
http://www.bizplancompetitions.com/

Very popular are the Hackathons, and HackNY.org has been at the forefront in organizing them. To learn more about HackNY, watch this video:
http://vimeo.com/40255931

The City of New York, through NYCEDC, is also involved in organizing business plan competitions. A notable one is NYC Next Idea, organized by NYCEDC's Center for Economic Transformation together with Columbia's Engineering School, aiming to attract teams from all over the world to relocate to New York: http://bit.ly/Vo7vSe

Another competition opened to entrepreneurs all over the world and organized by the city is NYC Venture Fellows: www.nycventurefellows.org

Another important appointment is BigApps, a contest organized by the City of New York for the best applications centered around the City, and for which the City makes available its own databases. http://challenges.nycbigapps.com

Accelerators, Incubators and Workspaces

New York is well supported by a variety of shared spaces, incubators and accelerators that can provide affordable office space and resources for ventures in a multitude of industry sectors. What is best for you depends on what business you are in and what kind of help you are seeking. The list of incubators, accelerators and co-working spaces has been constantly increasing. For an up-to-date list of co-working spaces, there are a number of sites one can consult, such as Mark Birch's blog or the CoWorkingNewYorkCity wiki: http://bit.ly/WYbSPM

Incubators/Accelerators
Some of these incubators and accelerators will help you in their own area of expertise. Some have a competitive admission process (e.g. Techstars) but offer some initial funding and exposure to mentors and investors.

New York State/New York City-associated

DUMBO Incubator	http://bit.ly/XGGyEh
ITAC (manufacturing)	http://www.itac.org/
NYC Seed	http://www.nycseed.com/
NYC ACRE (Energy)	http://www.nycacre.com/
NYSTAR (state programs)	http://esd.ny.gov/nystar/
Varick Street Incubator	http://bit.ly/WmxKGx

Tech Accelerator Programs

Betaworks	http://betaworks.com
DreamIt Ventures	http://dreamitventures.com/
Entrepreneurs Roundtable Acc.	http://eranyc.com/

FinTech Innovation Lab	www.fintechinnovationlab.com
First Growth Venture Network	www.firstgrowthvn.com
Founder Labs	http://www.founderlabs.org/
NYC Seed Seedcamp	http://bit.ly/XCgjht
TechStars NYC	http://www.techstars.org/nyc
Women Innovate Mobile	www.womeninnovatemobile.com

Health Care Accelerators
Blueprint Health	http://blueprinthealth.org/
NY Digital Health Acc.	http://digitalhealthaccelerator.com
StartUp Health Academy	http://www.startuphealth.com

Other Accelerators
| CFDA Fashion Incubator | http://bit.ly/SPg1Ye |
| Pratt Design Incubator | http://incubator.pratt.edu/ |

Digital Media/Technology Incubators
Alley NYC	http://www.alleynyc.com/
Astia (Women Entr.)	http://www.astia.org/
BMW iVentures	http://bit.ly/10N4RlR
Dogpatch Labs	http://dogpatchlabs.com
Founder's Institute	http://fi.co/
Grind Spaces	http://grindspaces.com/
Hatchery	http://www.hatchery.vc/
ingk labs	http://ingk.com/
InSITE	http://insiteny.org/
NEST	http://www.nestnewyork.com
Startl	http://startl.org/
Sunshine Bronx Incubator	http://sunshineny.com/bronx
Tipping Point Partners	http://bit.ly/10N5bB3
WeWorkLabs	http://weworklabs.com/

Shared Workspaces
3rd Ward	http://www.3rdward.com/
Bat Haus Bushwick	http://batha.us/
Bitmap Creative Labs	http://site.bitmapnyc.com/
Brooklyn Creative League	http://bit.ly/Yu0qjK
DUMBO Startup Lab	http://dumbostartuplab.com/
General Assembly	http://www.generalassemb.ly/
Green Desk	http://green-desk.com/
Greenpoint Coworking	http://greenpointcoworking.com/

Hive 55	http://www.hiveat55.com/
In Good Company	http://bit.ly/Yu0u39
New Work City	http://www.nwc.co/
Projective Space	http://www.projective.co/
Sunshine Suites	http://sunshineny.com/
Soho Haven	http://www.sohohaven.com/
Space 4 Work	http://space-4-work.com/
Tech Space	http://www.techspace.com/
The Makery	http://brooklyn.makery.org/
The Yard	http://workattheyard.com/
WECREATE NYC	http://www.wecreatenyc.com/
WeWork	http://www.weworknyc.com/
Wix Lounge	http://www.wixlounge.com/

Networking

There are many opportunities to network with companies, entrepreneurs and investors. There are multiple events in New York every night. Fortunately you can subscribe to a few newsletters that will help you keep track of what's going on. New York Tech Meetup is probably the best known of the regular events. 800+ tickets are sold every month to attend the event at the Skirball Auditorium at NYU and they are regularly sold out. You can also watch the event simulcast at other locations in New York or streamed on the web. Meetup is the company that provides the online infrastructure for all the meetup events, and on its site you can find a great number of meetings on a variety of subjects that fit your interests.

Newsletters
Gary's Guide publishes a list of upcoming events via a weekly newsletter, but on the web site you can also look at a list of classes and job opportunities:
www.garysguide.com/events?region=newyork
Charlie O'Donnell publishes a weekly newsletter of events from his blog:
www.thisisgoingtobebig.com/nycevents
Startup Digest also has a list of local events you can subscribe to.
http://startupdigest.com/new-york-city

Organizations—events, networking, mentoring, job opportunities

Columbia Venture Community	http://columbia.vc/
NY Venture Community	http://bit.ly/Y5xyKV
Meetup	http://www.meetup.com/

New York tech Meetup   http://nytm.org/
TiE, the global technology network   https://ny.tie.org/

Funding

There are a variety of investors in New York, from angel investors to early-stage and later-stage venture capitalists. You can also apply to and be funded by one of the accelerator programs in NY.

Angel Investors
Angels are individual investors who invest on their own or as a group. The typical investment size is $25k-100k per individual. They typically invest in the seed round and sometimes participate in follow-on rounds of financing. When acting as a group, you can expect investments of $200K and up.

The New York Angels is the largest angel organization in New York, comprising over 100 active individual investors. There are other organized groups, such as Golden Seeds, focused on women entrepreneurs, and there are many individual investors as well.

Golden Seeds   http://www.goldenseeds.com
New York Angels   http://newyorkangels.com

The largest directory of organized angel investor (and seed funding groups) is maintained by Gust, at: https://gust.com/find-investors

Seed/Early Stage Investors
Seed and early stage investors are groups investing funds in the early stages of a company's life. They might invest in seed rounds (like the angels and often together with angels) and they invest in "Series A" rounds. They typically keep investing in follow-on rounds. While amounts may vary greatly, typical investment size is between $250K-1M for a seed round and $1-3M for a Series A round.

Advancit Capital   http://www.advancitcapital.com/
Betaworks   http://www.betaworks.com/
Bold Start   http://www.boldstart.vc/
Boxgroup   http://www.boxgroupnyc.com/
Brooklyn Bridge Ventures http://bit.ly/14kDOSi
Contour Venture Partners http://www.contourventures.com/
DFJ Gotham Ventures   http://www.dfjgotham.com/
Eniac Ventures   http://eniac.vc/

ff Venture Capital	http://ffvc.com/
Firstmark Capital	http://firstmarkcap.com/
First Round Capital	http://www.firstround.com/
Greycroft	http://greycroft.com/
IA Ventures	http://www.iaventures.com/
Lerer Ventures	http://www.lererventures.com/
Founder Collective	http://foundercollective.com/
Great Oaks	http://www.greatoaksvc.com/
High Peaks Venture Partners	http://www.hpvp.com/
Metamorphic Ventures	http://metamorphic.vc/
NYC Seed	http://www.nycseed.com/
Quotidian Ventures	http://quotidianventures.com/
RTP Ventures	http://www.rtp.vc/
Tribeca Venture Partners	http://www.tribecavp.com/
Vaizra Seed Fund	http://www.vaizra.info/

Early Stage to Later Stage Investors
This group of investors typically does not invest in seed deals, but they may invest from early to later stage. Initial investments may vary, but over time they might invest between $5 and $15M over the life of a company.

Accel Partners	http://www.accel.com/
Bain Capital Ventures	http://bit.ly/Vdmj0B
Bessemer Venture Partners	http://www.bvp.com/
Canaan Partners	http://www.canaan.com/
Flybridge Capital partners	http://www.flybridge.com/
Insight Venture Partners	http://www.insightpartners.com/
Oak Investment Partners	http://www.oakvc.com/
Polaris Venture Partners	http://www.polarisventures.com/
Raptor Ventures	http://www.raptorventures.com/
RRE Ventures	http://www.rre.com/
Softbank Capital	http://bit.ly/TACSs2
Spark Capital	http://www.sparkcapital.com/
Starvest Partners	http://www.starvestpartners.com/
Union Square Ventures	http://www.usv.com/
Vedanta Capital	http://www.vedantacapital.com/
Venrock	http://www.venrock.com/

Strategic/Corporate
Corporate investors are venture capital arms of large corporations looking to invest in companies that can bring strategic value to their businesses

Aol Ventures	http://www.aolventures.com/
Bertelsmann	http://www.bdmifund.com/
Bloomberg Ventures	http://bloombergventures.com/
BMW i Ventures	http://bit.ly/10N4RlR
Citi Ventures	http://ventures.citi.com/
Time Warner Investments	http://bit.ly/10PDbgW

Specific Help for Foreign Entrepreneurs

One way to orient oneself when coming from outside the US is to contact the Division for International Business at the Mayor's Office for International Affairs located at the United Nations: www.nyc.gov/international

Other organizations that can help foreign entrepreneurs in New York are:
http://ventureoutny.com
http://worldwideinvestornetwork.com
www.meetup.com/NY-Tech-International

There are some organizations attached to the Chambers of Commerce of specific countries that do work on behalf of entrepreneurs.

Another resource working with international economic development agencies to help their nationals enter the US startup/tech scene is TechResources.us
http://www.techresources.us/content/about-us

For further updates, information and a continuing discussion on Tech and the City and the New York startup community, please go to:
http://www.tech-and-the-city.com

Acknowledgments

Without the help of many friends and the cooperation and patience of our families "Tech and the City" would not have been possible. We want to acknowledge our spouses, Glauco Maggi and Alexandra Giurgiu Piol, who are also our colleagues—Glauco, journalist for *La Stampa* and *Libero*; Alexandra, veteran venture capitalist—and have been valuable consultants both during the research and in writing the book.

Sara Matiz brought the perfect combination of New York startup and Italian design to our book cover (see below for more on her and her firm). We thank Sara and Simone Polga for all the good work.

Francesco Mogini, a brilliant student at the University of Pennsylvania (class of 2015), spent time with us as a summer intern and assisted in organizing the 50+ interviews the book is based on, and in transcribing the ones that were recorded. He became so passionate about the world of startups that he has now created his own, Cameio.

Maria Cristina Bianchi, who had a key role in helping us launch our book in Europe, and Elserino Piol, who is completely responsible (in joint venture with Marisa Piol) for the existence of one of the authors, gave us enthusiastic support for the Italian Edition.

Many other friends have given us support with comments and suggestions: Drew Hammond who was instrumental in helping us edit the book; Joyce Evans, who assisted us in the challenging task of getting an English and Italian edition out at the same time; Kelly Hoey, Richie Hecker and Dawn Barber for their invaluable advice and help; Alain Bankier, Evan Korth, Howard Morgan, Alan Patricof, David S. Rose, Foy Savas, Mark Stahlman, David Tisch, Fred Wilson, Chris Wiggins, who all took the time to read the book and give us feedback.

But most of all we want to thank all the entrepreneurs, investors, advisors, members of "Team Bloomberg" and everyone else who agreed to be interviewed or talked to us and gave us their precious views, recollections and anecdotes. This book is about them. They have made the New York ecosystem possible and have helped create the community that will make it sustainable. We list them in alphabetical order and hope we don't forget anyone: Alain Bankier, Dawn Barber, Arthur Bierer, John Borthwick, Bruno Cilio, Brian S. Cohen, Brendan Collins, Dennis Crowley, Mark Peter Davis, Zach Davis, Rohan Deuskar, Chris Dixon, Owen Davis, Esther Dyson, Elena Favilli, Yadilka Frias, Brian Frumberg, Gianluca Galletto, Maria Gotsch, Richie Hecker, Scott Heiferman, Kelly Hoey, Moshiko Hogeg, Cella Irvine, Don Katz, John Katzman, Richard Kennedy, Evan Korth, Micah Kotch, Scott Kurnit, Eric Litman, Tristan Louis, Josh Miller, Howard Morgan, Fernando Napolitano, Elio Narciso, Jerry Neumann, Alan Patricof, Michael Petrucelli, Dmytro Pokhylko, Adam Pritzker, Jeremy Robbins, David S. Rose, Davide Rossi, Adam Rothenberg, Kevin Ryan, Alessandro Santo, Veronika Sonsev, Boštjan Špetič, Mark Stahlman, Guy Story, Kristy Sundjaja, David Teten, David Tisch, Carlton Vann, Peter Weijmarshausen, Chris Wiggins, Fred Wilson, Joanne Wilson and Cheni Yerushalmi.

About the Book Cover

Sara-Mosele Matiz created our book cover. She is a New York-based Italian designer who recently won "NYC Best for Business Infographic Competition 2012," launched by the Mayor's office to represent New York as "the best place for business." Her Infographic (viewable at www.nycedc.com/competition) will be used to promote New York City in the world.

With an Architecture degree from the University of Venice, Sara has been living in New York since 1998. In 2002 she founded Matiz Architecture & Design (MAD) with her husband Juan Carlos Matiz (www.mad-nyc.com). Among her works, she has designed the interiors for some of New York's startups, including Etsy (http://bit.ly/VtKpav). Sara is also researching how startups' workspaces are different from the traditional ones: "I'm trying to understand how technology affects the way we communicate and collaborate at work, which generational differences are in play, and how graphics and design may be used to change the attitudes and behaviors of people, encouraging knowledge sharing, making business more agile, adaptable to change and sustainable." That is why Sara was the ideal designer for creating the cover of "Tech and the City."

About the Authors

Maria Teresa Cometto is an Italian journalist with more than 25 years in the media industry. Since 2000 she has been based in New York, covering business, financial markets and high-tech, and writing for some of the most important Italian papers such as Corriere della Sera, which is the daily with the largest circulation in Italy, and Il Mondo, the most authoritative Italian business magazine. She is well known for her articles on the US technology industry and for her many interviews with leading economists, including 14 Nobel Laureates. Maria is also the author of several books, among which Figli & Soldi ("Kids & Money," 2008). Twitter: @mtcometto

Alessandro Piol is a New York-based venture capitalist and angel investor with over 30 years of experience in the technology industry. Alessandro is a Partner and co-founder of Vedanta Capital. Previously he was a General Partner of Invesco Private Capital where he headed the technology practice. Prior to joining Invesco, Alessandro spent 10 years with AT&T where he co-founded AT&T Ventures, the venture capital arm of AT&T where he focused on early-stage new media investments, as well as Pixel Machines, an AT&T-backed startup in the graphics super-computing business. Alessandro is President of the New York chapter of TiE, a global organization fostering entrepreneurship; he serves on the Entrepreneurial Advisory Board and the Board of Visitors of the Fu Foundation School of Engineering at Columbia University; and he is a mentor, advisor or board member of various private companies. He received an BS and MS in Computer Science from Columbia University and an MBA from the Harvard Business School. Twitter: @ilmago

Notes

Throughout the book we have footnoted reference to articles, areas that would benefit from more information or explanation, as well as links to the startups mentioned in the book. Web sites and links already provided in the last section of the book, "A Startup Guide to New York," are not necessarily included. To access the notes online, up-to-date and with live links, please go to: http://tech-and-the-city.com/Notes/ or simply scan the QR code above with your smartphone or tablet.

Chapter 1

[1] Look at Lazerow's video here: http://bit.ly/WIaH9k

[2] NYNMA's original board was composed by Brian Horey, Mark Stahlman, Sunny Bates, Red Burns, Connie Connors, Cella Irvine, Jerry Michalski, Michael Wheeler, and Alessandro Piol. Over the following years, several other notables from the NY Tech scene joined the board, including Alain Bankier, Edith C. Bjornson, Nick Butterworth, Donna Campbell, Eric Goldberg, Howard Greenstein, Craig Kanarick, Ann Kirschner, Stefanie Syman, Andrew Weinreich. The first executive director of NYNMA was Lori Schwab, who was followed by Alice O'Rourke. Part of the team managing NYNMA included Ellen Auwarter, Dawn Barber (co-founder of NY Tech Meetup), Anita Fowler, Sherry Riesner, Brian Rosenberg and several others.

[3] Michael Maiello, "The Futurist," *Forbes*, Dec 22, 2003, http://onforb.es/XhzM7p

[4] For more color, please see: Janet Stites, "At Cybersuds events, members of New York's new-media community look for partners, strategic or otherwise," *The New York Times*, Nov 23, 2998, http://nyti.ms/XoKScG

[5] Michael Krantz, "The Great Manhattan Geek Rush of 1995," *New York*, Nov 13, 1995, p.36. Available online at Google Books: http://bit.ly/Xr3B5o

[6] Fred Wilson, "Sixteen Years Ago," *A VC: musings of a VC in NYC*, June 7,2012, http://bit.ly/11sOeSl

[7] For some history on Jason Calacanis and his Silicon Alley magazine (at the time of its demise) please read: Amy Harmon, "Requiem for a Cheerleader: Silicon Alley Magazine Is Dead," *The New York Times*, Oct 8, 2001, http://nyti.ms/XkSRd5

[8] Donald Katz, *Just Do It: The Nike Spirit in the Corporate World*, (Random Hose, 1994)

Chapter 2

[1] You can watch a short video on TheGlobe.com on YouTube: "A Very Public Offering: The Story of TheGlobe.com," *Public*, http://bit.ly/15fM5s7

[2] The documentary is currently (February 2013) available on Netflix and you can watch a trailer at http://bit.ly/12lx34H

[3] Otto Friedrich, Michael Moritz, J. Madeleine Nash and Peter Stoler, "Machine of the Year: The Computer Moves In," *Time*, Jan 3, 1983, http://bit.ly/YuK05k

Chapter 3

[1] Michael Bloomberg and Matthew Winkler, *Bloomberg by Bloomberg* (John Wiley & Sons, 1997)

[2] For excerpts of the speech, see http://on.nyc.gov/UsAzC4

[3] *Forbes Magazine*, Sept 19, 2012, http://onforb.es/VLRKz2

[4] *New York Times, City Room Column*, Sept 24, 2009, http://nyti.ms/VtqiqC

[5] Joyce Purnick, *Mike Bloomberg: Money, Power, Politics* (PublicAffairs, 2009)

[6] NPR, *New York City's Mayor is a Geek at Heart*, Apr 6, 2012, http://n.pr/105hkqh

[7] Michael Bloomberg and Matthew Winkler, *Bloomberg by Bloomberg* (John Wiley & Sons, 1997)

[8] Ibid.

[9] Ibid.

[10] Edward Glaeser, "The Reinventive City," *City Journal*, July 13, 2009, http://bit.ly/ZsloQ7

[11] Ibid.

[12] Mayor Bloomberg's remarks at press conference on term limits, Oct 2, 2008, http://on.nyc.gov/114QwFV

[13] Brian S. Cohen and John Kador, *What Every Angel Investor Wants You to Know: An Insider Reveals How to Get Smart Funding for Your Billion Dollar Idea*, (McGraw-Hill, 2013).

[14] http://now.cornell.edu/nyctech/

[15] Conor O'Clery, *The Billionaire Who Wasn't: How Chuck Feeney Made and Gave Away a Fortune Without Anyone Knowing*, (PublicAffairs, 2007)

[16] Fred Wilson, "A look back at Summize," *A VC: musings of a VC in NYC*, Apr 20, 2010, http://bit.ly/VUKBgF

[17] Fred Wilson, "A look back at Summize," *A VC: musings of a VC in NYC*, Apr 20, 2010, http://bit.ly/VUKBgF

[18] Matt Linley, "The Man Who Built Twitter's Tech Team Is About To Start Building Up New York's Tech Scene," *Business Insider,* May 23, 2012, http://read.bi/Y1gXLO

[19] Richard Pérez-Peña, "Cornell Alumnus Is Behind $350 Million Gift to Build Science School in City," *The New York Times,* December 19, 2011, http://nyti.ms/13pAQfP

[20] New York City press release announcing the new Cornell campus, Dec 19, 2011, http://on.nyc.gov/10qbFew

[21] Joyce Purnick, *Mike Bloomberg: Money, Power, Politics* (PublicAffairs, 2009)

[22] Dan Senor and Saul Singer, *Startup Nation: The Story of Israel's Economic Miracle* (Twelve, Hachette Group, 2009)

[23] Christopher Dickey, "Roosevelt Island: New York Tech Hub," *Newsweek*, July 30, 2012, http://thebea.st/WPlEld

[24] Richard Pérez-Peña, "Cornell Alumnus Is Behind $350 Million Gift to Build Science School in City," *The New York Times*, December 19, 2011, http://nyti.ms/13pAQfP

[25] "Mayor Bloomberg and Cornell University announce applications for new 'beta' class" *NYC.gov* press release, Aug 22, 2012, http://on.nyc.gov/V700Pk

[26] Matt Linley, "The Man Who Built Twitter's Tech Team Is About To Start Building Up New York's Tech Scene," *Business Insider*, May 23, 2012, http://read.bi/Y1gXLO

[27] The suffix at the end of an Internet address such as ".com" and ".org."

[28] The City of New York "New York City's Digital Roadmap: Progress & Innovation," August 2012, p.51. Please see http://on.nyc.gov/W43JZZ and download the .pdf file at: http://on.nyc.gov/VYyFwN

Chapter 4

[1] "High Tech Boom Town," *New York*, Nov 13, 1995, http://bit.ly/X8Oqlg

[2] To see the famous picture, please go to: http://bit.ly/XMwhJW. Incidentally, the high-rise building next door, the Madison Green apartment building, was the site of the world's first computerized real estate sales office, designed by David S. Rose in 1982, as described in *Infoworld* of March 14, 1983: http://bit.ly/X1yddD

[3] "The Most Active Venture Capital Firms," *Crain's New York Business*, Feb 17, 2012.

[4] David D. Kirkpatrick, "Flatiron Grip," *New York*, Sep 20, 1999, http://nym.ag/YNzSpw

[5] Fred Wilson, "The Darwinian Evolution of Startup Hubs," *A VC: musings of a VC in NYC*, May 19, 2012, http://bit.ly/13Chhy5

[6] Fred Wilson, "Geocities," *A VC: musings of a VC in NYC*, Apr 24, 2009, http://bit.ly/XydjEd

[7] Hunch: http://hunch.com

[8] Tumblr: http://www.tumblr.com

9 Gilt Groupe: http://www.gilt.com; 10gen: http://www.10gen.com; Business Insider: http://www.businessinsider.com

10 Stylitics: http://www.stylitics.com

Chapter 5

1 Jon Steinberg, "Meatpacking District Walking Tour," *New York*, Aug 18, 2004, http://nym.ag/XfuNF4

2 Launch.it: http://launch.it

3 Branch: http://branch.com

4 Medialets: http://www.medialets.com

5 Abbie Fentress Swanson, "Google Building's Scaffolding Shows Chelsea's Past," WNYC, Apr 9, 2012, http://wny.cc/12PhkpS. For more information on the Local Law 11, about façade inspections, please see http://on.nyc.gov/X3UD2A

6 Google New York: http://bit.ly/14XR9jY and http://bit.ly/W0EsPv

7 Gust: http://www.gust.com

8 2Tor: http://2u.com; Noodle Education: http://www.noodle.org

Chapter 6

1 Matt Villano, "The Best Bar to … Rub Elbows With a VC: Tom & Jerry's," *Entrepreneur*, June 21, 2011, http://bit.ly/XVqsIC

2 Foursquare: https://foursquare.com

3 Zemanta: http://www.zemanta.com

4 Mobli: http://www.mobli.com

5 Julia Boorstin, "How Second Market is Staying Relevant, Post-Facebook," *CNBC*, Aug 6, 2012, http://bit.ly/Yed4gz

6 SecondMarket: http://www.secondmarket.com

7 The Pebble watch: http://getinpulse.com

8 Kickstarter: http://www.kickstarter.com

Chapter 7

[1] More on the Brooklyn Tech Triangle study: http://bit.ly/XfCTNU

[2] For more on Brooklyn's transformation, see: Kay S. Hymowitz, "How Brooklyn Got Its Groove Back," *City Journal*, Autumn 2011, http://bit.ly/VpRCuX

[3] Huge: http://www.hugeinc.com; Big Spaceship: http://www.bigspaceship.com; Red Antler: http://www.redantler.com; Carrot Creative: http://carrotcreative.com; Spike DDB: http://www.spikeddb.com

[4] How About We: http://www.howaboutwe.com

[5] Dumbo Improvement District: http://dumbo.is

[6] Digital Dumbo events: http://www.digitaldumbo.com

[7] Docracy: http://www.docracy.com

[8] Chad Dickerson, "Funding Etsy's Future," *Etsy News Blog*, May 9, 2012, http://etsy.me/Xbi1uv

[9] Etsy: http://www.etsy.com

[10] Makerbot: http://www.makerbot.com

[11] Techshop: http://brooklyn.techshop.ws

Chapter 8

[1] Chris Arnade, "Sushine: Hunts Point Bronx," part of the photographic essay *Faces of Addiction*, http://bit.ly/XVASru

[2] *Ephemeral New York* Blog, Jul 28, 2012, http://bit.ly/XfGiML

[3] Mass Ideation: http://www.massideation.com; Think Work Media: http://thinkworkmedia.com; Yadilka: http://yadilka.com

Chapter 9

[1] Digital Natives Group: http://nativesgroup.com

[2] Queens Tech Meetup: http://www.meetup.com/queens-tech

NOTES

[3] To learn more about Fresh Direct: David Leonhardt, "Filling Pantries Without a Middleman," *The New York Times*, Nov 22, 2006, http://nyti.ms/12POaHs. Also: http://bit.ly/VWLpGK

[4] Shapeways: http://www.shapeways.com

Chapter 10

[1] Site of the Garibaldi-Meucci Museum: http://bit.ly/15k0XWo. Also see: http://bit.ly/YxjIPF

[2] Meucci Resolution at the House of Representatives: http://bit.ly/ZhoHKu

Chapter 11

[1] Brad Feld, *Startup Communities: Building an Entrepreneurial Ecosystem in Your City*, (Wiley, October 2012)

Chapter 12

[1] Tristan Louis, "Silicon Valley vs. New York: Social vs. Algorithms," *TNL.net*, Jan 8, 2011, http://bit.ly/XR2uis

Chapter 13

[1] For the press release, please see http://on.nyc.gov/UsAzC4

[2] NYPD Web Site, Crime Statistics, http://on.nyc.gov/10WJbVD

[3] Fred Wilson, "Metainstability," *A VC: musings of a VC in NYC,* Oct 4, 2012, http://bit.ly/YmySII

Chapter 14

[1] Alexandra Wilkis Wilson, *By Invitation Only: How We Built Gilt and Changed the Way Millions Shop* (Portfolio, 2012)

[2] Hannah Seligson, "Nurturing a Baby and a Start-Up Business," *The New York Times*, June 9, 2012, http://nyti.ms/UZcQ1a

243

Chapter 15

[1] Nassim N. Taleb, *The Black Swan*, (Random House, 2007)

[2] For an article on the history of fab.com, see http://onforb.es/YtBkvp

Chapter 16

[1] Source: press release of March 27, 2012 http://bit.ly/XzUhgJ

Chapter 18

[1] Jonathan Cole, *The Great American University: Its Rise to Preeminence, Its Indispensable National Role, Why It Must Be Protected*, (PublicAffairs, 2010)

[2] The third co-founder is Hilary Mason, now lead scientist at bit.ly and still an advisor to HackNY. To learn more about HackNY: **http://hackny.org**

[3] In addition, Evan Korth is on the board of New York Tech Meetup.

Chapter 22

[1] This is a great historic read: Gary Wolfe, "The (Second Phase of the) Revolution Has Begun," *Wired,* October 2004, http://bit.ly/13loZXA

Conclusions and Advice

[1] Some super articles that every entrepreneur should read:
Steve Blank: http://bit.ly/YmGWro
Elena Favilli: http://bit.ly/Y4XYuV
Paul Graham: http://bit.ly/ZeaWbk
Mark Suster: http://bit.ly/WgAQMt
Fred Wilson: http://bit.ly/VZvl5X and http://bit.ly/Zt2bsx (and many others)

Index

Made in the USA
Charleston, SC
30 April 2013